D1732724

Songs of Freedom
The James Connolly Songbook

James Connolly
Edited by Mat Callahan
Preface by Theo Dorgan
Foreword by James Connolly Heron

Mat Callahan

&

Yvonne Moore

1.29.2016

PMPRESS

Songs of Freedom: The James Connolly Songbook
James Connolly
Edited by Mat Callahan

© PM Press 2013
All rights reserved. No part of this book may be transmitted by any means without permission in writing from the publisher

PO Box 23912
Oakland, CA 94623
www.pmpress.org

Cover design by John Yates
Layout by Jonathan Rowland

ISBN: 978-1-60486-826-5
Library of Congress Control Number: 2013911514

10 9 8 7 6 5 4 3 2 1

Printed in the USA on recycled paper, by the Employee Owners of Thomson-Shore in Dexter, Michigan.
www.thomsonshore.com

Contents

---

1   Connolly did not identify the composer of the song, Claude Joseph Rouget de Lisle; see Connolly's note.
2   The Watchword and Watchword of Labor are the same song, according to the lyrics.

Preface
Great, Brave, Undaunted James Connolly

IN 1903, AGED 35, James Connolly applied for membership of the Socialist Labour Party of Great Britain. On the line marked "Occupation," he wrote: "Agitator."

At Christmas that same year, in New York, he wrote:

> 'Tis Christmas Day in Ireland and I am sitting here alone
> Three thousand miles of ocean intervene
> And the faces of my loved ones in my little Irish home
> Come glancing in and out my thoughts between.

"Agitator" was the blunt truth, because that is what Connolly set himself as a task: to agitate, to stir up, to raise dormant passions, to awaken a hunger and thirst for liberty and justice.

And at the same time, this sentimental, even mawkish verse shows a man capable of being stirred by an old-fashioned kind of loneliness, and reaching for a commonplace verse form to express his sentiments.

When a person's character exhibits this kind of swing, from blunt, pugnacious truthfulness to sentimental longing, we may be sure at the very least that here is a human being who shares with us a range of passions and foibles, who embodies perhaps real contradictions, who cannot, in any case, be reduced to a cipher.

The trouble with Connolly in our time is that he has become a hollow icon, a kind of ancestor figure to the Left, of no real substance to many who invoke his name save as a touchstone of legitimacy in a certain kind of politics.

Connolly the man, the family man, the ruthless organiser, the stern Union boss, the wounded martyr who loved a good song, the man who had good time for Yeats and Lady Gregory but who set up and led the Irish Citizen Army as a serious military force formed for armed revolution—that Connolly, that complex man, has been forgotten or buried under a hollow mask.

What Left politicians of the present moment, and I include the leaders of the Trade Union movement in this category, most assuredly do not want is a revolutionary politics of the kind that Connolly worked all his life to establish.

I do not say they are wrong: perhaps our politics has evolved to the point that what Connolly laboured for can be more readily achieved in a social democratic process, though I wonder if perhaps we have been waiting a little too long for evidence of this.

It seems to me disrespectful to the man's memory, to claim him in the name of a politics he did not profess. It seems to me more than a little unjust to neglect or elide the full human rounded character of the man as he actually was.

Gathering together these songs of Connolly's is a useful way of restating the man's essential humanity. Of the tunes, the borrowed ones are the best, and while I could not quarrel with the sentiments of the lyrics, I do quarrel with the fluffy sentimentality of the style. Then, tastes change, I must allow for that, and such reservations aside it seems to me valuable to have these songs in wider circulation, both as evidence of what was once thought and sung, and as a spur to make new the values and aspirations, the hopes and dreams that the songs most assuredly aim to embody.

Connolly did not set out to make his life as a songmaker, but his large heart saw the need to supply a want in the national life, a want of good songs that spoke of liberty and justice, that scorned slavery and injustice. He would be pleased, I think, to know how many such songs have entered into our repertoire, and how many are being written and sung today, and it may well be that he would gladly have left this side of the business to men and women with more talent for it than he possessed, had they been there for him to find.

James Connolly loved his wife and family, he pined for them when they were separated; he loved his class, perhaps more in the abstract than in the concrete, as he loved justice, as he loved to struggle, as he loved to agitate. All of these things he took very seriously, as he took songs, and poems, and the theatre seriously. When he wrote "We only want the Earth," he meant it. The earth, and all its fruits, its arts and pleasures as well as ownership of the means of production. I have no evidence for it, but I am certain he would have approved of "Bread and Roses" as a profound and delightful motto.

He was born in Edinburgh, he served seven years in the British Army, he gave seven years in the USA as a labour organiser, and he gave his life for this country that he loved, cheerfully as far as we know, certainly with full consciousness.

He knew us all too well: "Despite all seeming to the contrary we assert that Ireland is not really a revolutionary country. Ireland is a disaffected country which has long been accustomed to conduct constitutional agitation in revolutionary language, and what is worse, to conduct revolutionary movements with due regard to law and order."

And yet, it was for this country, for its poor and its powerless, that he laid down his life. Just as he wrote these songs to put heart into working men and women throughout the world.

Perhaps we might do him the honour of thinking about his real life? Perhaps we might stir ourselves from our glib invocations of a plaster saint and consider carefully and with respect his life as he actually lived it, his values and his writings?

With a song or two of Connolly's on our lips, we might well begin by considering these fateful words: "Ireland without her people means nothing to me."

Theo Dorgan,
Dublin 2012
Songs of Freedom Project

Foreword

Comrades,

I am delighted and consider it a great honour to be given this opportunity to contribute in a small way to this worthy and timely project in tribute to my great-grandfather.

The original *James Connolly Songbook* was based on a selection of songs performed in 1919 by comrades of Connolly to commemorate the anniversary of his birth. The concert was to take place in the Mansion House but was banned by the authorities, necessitating a move to the Trades Hall nearby. The concert went ahead. While police and workers clashed on the street outside, the singing of revolutionary songs could be heard from within the building. This mirrored, of course, songs sung by the volunteers during the course of The Rising, most notably the defiant singing of "The Soldiers' Song" as they fled the burning GPO.

Such is the power of song.

Congratulations and thanks are due to all involved in this enterprise. It is entirely fitting that the project takes place on the centenary of the 1913 lock out. I am the proud holder of a medal presented to my great-grandfather in the aftermath of that great event by the Independent Labour Party of Ireland marked "Dublin Labour War 1913–1914" and bearing the inscription "A Felon's Cap is the Noblest Crown an Irish Head Can Wear."

The men and women of that time were our golden generation. Among their number were poets, playwrights, artists, teachers, actors, and musicians marking the coming together of three great movements—the national, the labour, and the cultural. It is, therefore, entirely fitting and in keeping with that spirit and tradition that we remember and celebrate 1913 in song.

My grand-aunt Nora Connolly, in her book *We Shall Rise Again*, said of rebel songs: "For more may be remembered of a country's history and treasured deep in the heart of a people through a song or a poem than through the pages of a history book"—how true.

It was Nora who taught singers her father's songs. "After 1916," she said, "I never did any more singing."—how sad.

Now with this project and through the great talent and commitment of all involved we can hear Nora sing again.

And so in gratitude I salute Mat, Joe, and all who contributed to this historic, worthy, and worthwhile project and in so doing trust it is not out of order to pay tribute to all of you at this time by stating, "Never had a man or woman a grander cause; never was a cause more grandly served."

Fraternally,
James Connolly Heron

Introduction

THE SONGS IN this volume speak for themselves. Even for those unfamiliar with James Connolly, the lyrics he either wrote or gathered together from other sources make abundantly clear their revolutionary, working-class, and internationalist intent. Furthermore, the introductions to each of the three separate books contained herein eloquently convey the reasons they were originally published. What needs explanation, however, is how the present volume came to be published, why there are three books joined together under the title *Songs of Freedom*, and the journey of discovery that led not only to the printed material but to the music on the accompanying CD.

It so happens that I was born on July 14, Bastille Day, the inaugural battle of the great French Revolution. When my sixtieth birthday was approaching in 2011, I decided that now, more than ever, it was necessary to celebrate revolution by singing revolutionary songs. Since many of my closest friends are Irish, I thought it most appropriate to sing Irish revolutionary songs. This was partly due to familiarity with such songs, but more importantly it was a response to the devastating effects of the financial crisis on Ireland. So I started assembling a repertoire. While there are literally thousands of wonderful songs available, my focus soon turned to the figure of James Connolly. There are several reasons for this, some personal, others historical, still others of a political nature. I had heard the name of Connolly spoken with reverence in my childhood. In fact, my brother was named James after Connolly. I had read *Portrait of a Rebel Father* in my youth and long held dear the principles of working-class solidarity, socialism, and national liberation for which Connolly

1

fought and died.[1] I recalled Connolly's famous statement regarding the necessity for the "joyous, defiant singing of revolutionary songs," without which there could be no revolutionary movement worthy of the name. I remembered that statement was taken from the introduction to a book of Connolly's called *Songs of Freedom*. But where to find this book? My search led me to a bookstore in Cong, County Mayo, where a diligent bookseller advised me that the only existing copy of *Songs of Freedom* was in the National Library in Dublin. But I needed it now, and I lived in Bern, Switzerland. What could I do? The bookseller kindly offered to locate another book he knew of which contained Connolly's songs. He eventually found one in a bookstore in London. I purchased this old, battered copy of *The James Connolly Songbook*, published by the Cork Workers Club, and began looking for the musical accompaniment.

Collaborating in this search were my dear friends Joe McHugh and Alan Burke, who had agreed to join me and several other musician friends in performing at my birthday party. Joe, Alan, and I were able to locate some of the tunes referred to under the titles of the songs in the songbook but we could not find them all, and time was pressing. It became clear that new music would have to be composed if we were to achieve our purpose of presenting a program featuring Connolly's lyrics. The result was a combination: some of the tunes Connolly originally used, some with music I composed and the band arranged. In addition, we added well-known songs about Connolly and one, by Jim Connell, that was obviously among Connolly's favorites, "The Red Flag."

The performance was a rousing success. Joe and Alan had the inspired idea that we do a proper job recording the music and put it out along with a new version of *The James Connolly Songbook*. This was more timely than ever, they argued, particularly given the dire conditions facing the Irish people, not to mention those in many countries facing similar catastrophes. Undertaking such a project required some research, however. We needed to consult with others more knowledgeable than ourselves on matters both current and historical. How would such an effort be received and how could it be realized? I decided it was necessary to go to the National Library in Dublin and see for myself the original *Songs of Freedom*.

What I found was a revelation. *Songs of Freedom* was published in America, not in Ireland. It was, Connolly wrote in his introduction, "offered until some one with greater means shall present to the American Working Class a more suitable collection, drawn not from the store of one nation alone, but from the Socialist poetry of the World." Even more striking was the fact that *Songs of Freedom* differed in important ways from *The James Connolly Songbook* with which we'd been working. As readers of the present volume will see, the original *Songs of Freedom* contains eighteen songs, nine of which are by Connolly, while *The James Connolly Songbook* contains twenty-three songs and poems, nineteen of which are by Connolly. Furthermore, the introductions to the two books are completely different. The introduction to the second book begins with the famous quote, referred to earlier, from Connolly's introduction to *Songs of Freedom* but it goes on to describe a concert held in Dublin in 1919 to celebrate Connolly's birth. It was the "selection of songs and recitation" to be performed at that concert which make up the contents of the Cork Workers Club book.

The story doesn't end there, however. A supporter of the present project, residing in San Francisco, U.S.A., put me in touch with Jim Lane of Cork, Ireland, who, I soon discovered, had been a member of the Cork Workers Club, was responsible for the publication of *The James Connolly Songbook*, and indeed had written the introduction to it. Furthermore, the songs appearing only in the songbook and not in the original *Songs of Freedom* had been patiently gathered from various pamphlets and newspapers in which they had appeared, one by one, over many years. Jim went on to explain that the inspiration for the songbook lay in yet another long lost manuscript: the 1919 *Connolly Souvenir* program for the concert described in the introduction to *The James Connolly Songbook* of 1972 (a second version was published in 1980). If that weren't enough, Jim photocopied this program and sent it to me. When I received it I was astounded. This important document has, along with *Songs of Freedom*, been virtually unavailable for almost a century. Were it not for the efforts of the Cork Workers Club, its contents would have been buried along with it. I knew in an instant that these three documents needed to be republished together, in one book, so that a new generation could see for themselves the words of James Connolly and those of his comrades, as they first appeared. The introduction to *The James Connolly Songbook* is, furthermore, indispensable for understanding the circumstances surrounding the Dublin concert of 1919, an historic event in its own right. In combination, then, these three books tell a much larger tale, international in scope and enduring in impact. *Songs of Freedom* was produced for and distributed to the working class in the United States. The *Connolly Souvenir* emerged three years after Connolly's execution as the Irish War of Independence was raging. The Cork Workers Club book was first published as "The Troubles" were unfolding in Northern Ireland. Connolly's ideas, especially his articulation of the need for a workers' republic, free not only from Britain but from capitalism under any flag, rang out through all these different and shifting circumstances. They remain the single most important purpose this new book hopes to serve. In short: read Connolly. He speaks as eloquently today as he did a century ago, his analysis and prescriptions for what ails humanity as visionary and practical as ever.

Reading Connolly

James Connolly is a hero to workers and oppressed people everywhere. Born in Edinburgh in 1868 and martyred by the British Government in 1916, his forty-eight years were devoted to the liberation of humanity from all forms of slavery.[2] Reading about Connolly is therefore necessary to understanding the world at the end of the 19th century and the beginning of the 20th. But even if you know nothing of Connolly's life, even if you are not familiar with Irish history or labor history, there are compelling reasons to read what Connolly wrote. As extraordinary as his personal leadership was, it is ultimately his ideas that are of the greatest import for present and succeeding generations. This new version of Songs of Freedom hopes to renew a dialogue with Connolly's writings starting with his poetic expression. But it mustn't end there. Connolly wrote several important books including *Labour in Irish History*, *Labour, Nationality and Religion*, and *Socialism Made Easy*.

He wrote extensively for numerous periodicals, including *The Harp* and *Workers' Republic.* One can find these writings on the internet and in collections available in bookstores (see bibliography).

A few short examples demonstrate the usefulness of Connolly's method of analysis and the accuracy of his predictions. In 1897 Connolly confronted illusions fostered by an outmoded and naïve view of "independence" from Britain:

> If you remove the English army tomorrow and hoist the green flag over Dublin castle, unless you set about the organization of the Socialist Republic your efforts would be in vain.
>
> England would still rule you. She would rule you through her capitalists, through her landlords, through her financiers, through the whole array of commercial and individualist institutions she has planted in this country and watered with the tears of our mothers and the blood of our martyrs.
>
> England would still rule you to your ruin, even while your lips offered hypocritical homage at the shrine of that Freedom whose cause you had betrayed.

Furthermore, Connolly clearly articulated what the Socialist Republic consisted of. The Programme of the Irish Socialist Republican Party[3] first published in 1896 begins:

> OBJECT
>
> Establishment of AN IRISH SOCIALIST REPUBLIC based upon the public ownership by the Irish people of the land, and instruments of production, distribution and exchange. Agriculture to be administered as a public function, under boards of management elected by the agricultural population and responsible to them and to the nation at large. All other forms of labour necessary

to the well-being of the community to be conducted on the same principles.

PROGRAMME

As a means of organising the forces of the Democracy in preparation for any struggle which may precede the realisation of our ideal, of paving the way for its realisation, of restricting the tide of emigration by providing employment at home, and finally of palliating the evils of our present social system, we work by political means to secure the following measures:

1.   Nationalisation of railways and canals.

2.   Abolition of private banks and money-lending institutions and establishments of state banks, under popularly elected boards of directors, issuing loans at cost.

3.   Establishment at public expense of rural depots for the most improved agricultural machinery, to be lent out to the agricultural population at a rent covering cost and management alone.

4.   Graduated income tax on all incomes over £400 per annum in order to provide funds for pensions to the aged, infirm and widows and orphans.

5.   Legislative restriction of hours of labour to £48 per week and establishment of a minimum wage.

6.   Free maintenance for all children.

7.   Gradual extension of the principle of public ownership and supply to all the necessaries of life.

8. Public control and management of National schools by boards elected by popular ballot for that purpose alone.

9. Free education up to the highest university grades.

10. Universal suffrage.

Reading these statements in light of the latest crisis of capitalism we must, at the very least, acknowledge that the outcome Connolly predicted has indeed occurred and might have been averted by enacting the proposals he advanced. No doubt, there is much to amend or alter due to changing circumstances but such principles as public ownership, public education for all, and the abolition of private banks demand our reconsideration today. Not only do they stand in opposition to ruling dogma, they provide a useful starting point for any discussion of alternative means of social organization. And these are only two examples from a much larger body of work covering themes as varied as religion, women's emancipation, military tactics, culture, and national liberation. In every sphere, Connolly's analysis contains not only consistent reasoning but genuinely novel insights. While rooted in revolutionary socialist thought, especially that of Karl Marx, Connolly applied himself to problems with an inventiveness and originality that could never be mistaken for the dogmatic or doctrinaire. This, too, should inspire us to unleash our own creativity applied to age-old problems.

Addressing the issue of the imperialist war about to break out in Europe in 1914, Connolly could have been speaking of today's imperial adventures in Afghanistan or Iraq: "If these men must die, would it not be better to die in their own country fighting for freedom for their class, and for the abolition of war, than to go forth to strange countries and die slaughtering and slaughtered by their own brothers that tyrants and profiteers might live?" In a manner strikingly similar to today's "clash of civilizations" rhetoric, imperialism's apologists were then loudly trumpeting a War for Civilization. Connolly's response is as persuasive now as it was a century ago:

Civilization cannot be built upon slaves; civilization cannot be secured if the producers are sinking into misery; civilization is lost if they whose labour makes it possible share so little of its fruits that its fall can leave them no worse than its security.

The workers are at the bottom of civilized society. That civilization may endure they ought to push upward from their poverty and misery until they emerge into the full sunlight of freedom. When the fruits of civilization, created by all, are enjoyed in common by all, then civilization is secure. Not till then.

About the Music

When we set about preparing the music to accompany Connolly's texts, we had at our disposal some old recordings, internet sources such as YouTube, and personal memory. We had no idea that the *Connolly Souvenir* program of 1919 even existed, let alone that it contained musical notation for the songs. *The James Connolly Songbook* only reproduced the lyrics and the names of the tunes or airs to which Connolly set his lyrics, so that's all we had to go on. But we took encouragement from Connolly himself. Connolly had often used popular tunes as the basis for his lyrics, many of which were not even Irish and certainly not traditional. Besides, as the introduction to *The James Connolly Songbook* states, "as many of these airs have long passed on in public memory, we suggest that where possible, workers should adapt his songs to the airs of today's popular songs and ballads."

This also presented a difficulty. Connolly's lyrics do not lend themselves easily to today's popular songs. They are readily comprehensible as texts but as song lyrics they require music designed to support their own rhythm and rhyme. The challenge, therefore, was to produce music that would make these lyrics singable by anyone while at the same time retaining melodic interest. Above all, the music had to convey the emotion intended by the text. The listener will have to judge how well we succeeded.

In conclusion, I need to emphasize that this book and accompanying CD are the result of a collective effort involving many people from several countries. I have already mentioned the crucial contribution of Joe McHugh and Alan Burke. To this must be added all the musicians and technicians who participated in making the music. None were "hired guns," and all gave their talent and labor to bring this message to the world. Initial financial support came from a circle of friends in Bern, Switzerland. The Cantons of Bern and Schaffhausen provided arts funding. Subsequently, appeals in San Francisco and Northern California gathered support from a diverse group that included labor unions, political activists, artists, and educators. It is a testament to the power of Connolly's vision that so many people from such different backgrounds have been inspired to call it to life in the 21st century.

Notes:

1. *A Portrait of a Rebel Father* is a book written by Nora Connolly O'Brien, Connolly's daughter, and published in 1935.

2. In the *Connolly Souvenir* of 1919 it is incorrectly stated that Connolly was born in Clones, County Monaghan, Ireland in 1870. This was legend and lore—and apparently never corrected by Connolly himself—but it was disproved once and for all by C. Desmond Greaves, who in his great biography, *The Life and Times of James Connolly*, presents the evidence. Greaves unearthed the birth records that confirm that Connolly's parents emigrated from County Monaghan to Edinburgh where James was born and raised.

3. At the head of the Programme was the famous epigram: "The great appear great because we are on our knees. Let us rise!" Connolly quoted this often but it did not originate with him or with James Larkin upon whose statue in Dublin it is inscribed. It is attributed to French revolutionary Camille Desmoulins.

The reader will notice that there are numerous hand-written corrections in the original Songs of Freedom. *We decided to leave them as we found them when copying the book in the National Library, Dublin. Perhaps these are Connolly's own corrections, although we were unable to establish that as of the present publication. Most important is that what is preserved here is an exact replica of one of the few remaining copies of* Songs of Freedom.

THE "TAKE AND HOLD" SONG BOOK

SONGS OF FREEDOM

BY

IRISH AUTHORS

DEDICATED TO THE
INDUSTRIAL AND
POLITICAL MOVE-
MENT FOR THE
EMANCIPATION OF
THE WORKING
CLASS . . . . . .

WITH AN INTRODUCTION

BY

JAMES CONNOLLY

PRICE · · · FIVE CENTS

PUBLISHED BY
J. E. C. DONNELLY
202 EAST 48TH STREET
NEW YORK

ERRATUM

Page 9—The tune to which song "Freedom of Labor" is set should be "The March of the Cameron Men."

Page 13—First line, for "Hurts" read "Hosts."

THE "TAKE AND HOLD" SONG BOOK

SONGS OF FREEDOM

BY

IRISH AUTHORS

DEDICATED TO THE
INDUSTRIAL AND
POLITICAL MOVE-
MENT FOR THE
EMANCIPATION OF
THE WORKING
CLASS . . . . . .

WITH AN INTRODUCTION

BY

JAMES CONNOLLY

PUBLISHED BY
J. E. C. DONNELLY
202 EAST 48TH STREET
NEW YORK

13

Introduction.

This little book of revolutionary songs is published for a two-fold purpose. First, it is in response to the belief of the Editor that ̶i̶n̶ no revolutionary movement is complete without its poetical expression. If such a movement has caught hold of the imagination of the masses they will seek a vent in song for the aspirations, the fears and the hopes, the loves and the hatreds engendered by the struggle. Until the movement is marked by the joyous, defiant, singing of revolutionary songs, it lacks one of the most distinctive marks of a popular revolutionary movement, it is the dogma of a few, and not the faith of the multitude. In this belief this small bouquet of songs, culled from a very limited garden, is offered until some one with greater means shall present to the American Working Class a more suitable collection, drawn not from the store of one nation alone, but from the Socialist poetry of the World. The propogandist effect of such a volume of songs with their proper musical setting, would be simply incalculable.

The second purpose of this volume may be readily guessed by a glance at its contents. It will be seen that every song herein contained was written by an Irishman.

This is in no spirit of insularity, but rather is meant as an encouragement to other Irishmen and women, to take their part and do their share in the upbuilding of the revolutionary movement of the Working Class. Most of these songs were written in Ireland, by men actually engaged in the revolutionary struggle of their time, whatever ruggedness may attach to their numbers is due to the fact that they were born in the stress and strain of the fight, and not in the scholarly seclusion of the study.

In conclusion, if this venture meets approval, we will carry our next into the field of recitative poetry, where a rich Irish harvest awaits the gleaner.

Editor.

3

THE WATCHWORD.

"Take and Hold."
O, hear ye the watchword of Labor.
  The slogan of they who'd be free,
That no more to any enslaver
  Must Labor bend suppliant knee.
That we on whose shoulders are borne
  The pomp and the pride of the great,
Whose toil they repaid with their scorn,
  Should meet it at last with our hate.

Chorus.

Then send it afar on the breeze, boys,
  That watchword, the grandest we've known,
That Labor must rise from its knees, boys,
  And take the broad earth as its own.

Aye, we who oft won by our valor,
  Empire for our rulers and lords,
Yet knelt in abasement and squalor
  To that we had made by our swords.
Now valor with worth will be blending,
  When, answering Labor's command,
We arise from the earth and ascending
  To manhood, for Freedom take stand.

Chorus.

Then out from the field and the city,
  From workshop, from mill and from mine,
Despising their wrath and their pity,
  We workers are moving in line.
To answer the watchword and token
  That Labor gives forth as its own,
Nor pause till our fetters we've broken,
  And conquered the spoiler and drone.
Chorus.
JAMES CONNOLLY.

THE RIGHTS OF MAN.

(From "Paddy's Resources," a song book of the
  Irish Revolutionists of 1798.)
Tune—"My Country 'Tis of Thee."
God save the rights of man,
Give him a heart to scan,
  Blessings so dear;
Let them be spread around,
Wherever man is found,
And with the welcome sound
  Ravish his ear.

4

See from the universe
Darkness and clouds disperse;
    Mankind, awake.
Reason and truth appear,
Freedom advances near,
Tyrants with terror hear,
    See how they quake.

Chorus.

Long have we felt the stroke,
Long have we borne the yoke,
    Sluggish and tame.
But a new era shines,
Enlightening all darkened minds,
Spreading to distant climes,
    Liberty's flame.

Let us as men agree,
And bid the world be free,
    Leading the way.
Should tyrants all conspire,
Fearless of sword and fire,
Freedom shall ne'er retire,
    Freedom shall sway.

THE SYMBOL.

Tune—"God Save Ireland."

With the symbol and the sign,
Rank on rank, and line on line,
True Pioneers of Liberty, we come.
Light for all the blind we bear,
Thunder so the deaf may hear,
And true Pentecostal fires for the dumb.

Chorus.

Forward, to Liberty advancing,
Forward, to Freedom from the thrall,
Come with willing heart and hand,
All who bear a common brand,
With the blood-red flag of Freedom over all.

Upward yet and onward still
To the city on the hill,
No rest we know till Labor has its own,
Till the death knell we have tolled,
Of the clinging curse of gold,
And the might of man o'er man is overthrown.

JOHN LESLIE.

5

BIDE YOUR TIME.

By M. J. BARRY.

(Prominent in the Irish Insurrectionary Movement of 1848.)

Bide your time, the morn is breaking
   Bright with Freedom's blessed ray,
Millions from their trance awaking,
   Soon shall stand in firm array.
Man shall fetter man no longer,
   Liberty shall march sublime,
Every moment makes us stronger,
Calm and thoughtful, bide your time.

Bide your time, one false step taken
   Perils all you yet have done,
Undismayed, erect, unshaken,
   Watch and wait and all is won.
Tis not by a rash endeaver,
   Man can e'er to greatness climb,
Would you win your rights forever?
   Firm, unshrinking, bide your time.

Bide your time, your worst transgression
   Were to strike and strike in vain,
He whose arm would smite oppression,
   Must not need to strike again.
Danger makes the brave man steady,
   Rashness is the coward's crime,
Be for Freedom's battle ready,
   When it comes, but bide your time.

STANDARD OF FREEDOM.

Unfold, Father Time, thy long records unfold,
Of noble achievements accomplished of old;
When men by the standard of liberty led,
Undauntedly conquered or cheerfully bled.

As spring to the fields, or as dew to the flower,
To the earth parched with heat, as the soft
   dropping shower,
As health to the wretch that lies languid and
   wan,
Or as rest to the weary—is Freedom to man.

When Freedom, the light of her countenance
   gives,
There only he revels, there only he lives,
Seize then the glad moment, and hail the decree
That bids millions rejoice and the nation be
   free.
                 IRELAND, 1798.

6

WHEN LABOR CALLS.

Tune—"Transvaal Volkslied or National
Anthem."

When Labor calls her children forth
    A waiting world to win,
Earth's noblest breed, true men of worth,
    Her ranks shall enter in.
Then, comrades all, prepare that we
    May hear that call anon,
And drive the hosts of tyranny
    Like clouds before the dawn,
            And drive our foes,
            And drive our foes,
    Our foes like clouds before the dawn.

Then knowest long has Labor groaned,
    A robbed and beaten thrall,
Whilst capital on high enthroned
    Reigned, lording over all.
But knowledge came and to the slave
    His power at last revealed,
He stands erect, his heart is brave,
    The tyrants doom is sealed.
            His doom is sealed,
            His doom is sealed,
    Thy tyrant's doom at last is sealed.

We work and wait till womb of Time
    Shall give fair Freedom birth,
To Labor's host, that hope sublime,
    Regenerates the earth.
And by that hope we toilers fired
    To nobler deeds shall be
That we may guide, by it inspired,
    Our class to Liberty.
            To Liberty,
            To Liberty,
    To guide our class to Liberty.

                    JAMES CONNOLLY.

HYMN TO FREEDOM.

Tune—"The Holy City."

Here at her altar kneeling,
    Sweet Freedom we adore,
And swear to hold her honor
    As sacred as of yore
Did all her holy martyrs,
    When, recking life as naught,
They went to death to guard the faith
    Her lore to man had brought.

18

Chorus.
O, Freedom, O, Freedom,
    Thy worshippers are we,
Here, kneeling, our allegiance,
    We render unto thee.

And as our fathers prayed to see
    The glories of her face,
We, kneeling at her altar,
    Beseech her longed-for grace,
She needs no gory sacrifice,
    Laid on her altar stones,
Our pilgrimage of poverty
    For all our faults atones.

She comes not clothed in majesty,
    No terrors in her tone,
Her priesthood is of Labor,
    Her service is our own.
To toil, and pain, and penury,
    Wherever manhood dwells,
She speaks, and lo, responsive,
    The heart of Labor swells.
She builds her altar in our hearts,
    Her ritual on our lives,
And they who yield her service
    Need not the grace that shives.

                    JAMES CONNOLLY.

FREEDOM'S PIONEERS.

Air—"Boys of Wexford."
Our feet upon the upward path
    Are set, where none may tread
Save those who to the rich man's wrath
    Dare turn rebellious head,
And hearts as brave; no cringing slave
    In all our rank appears;
Our proudest boast, in Labour's host,
    We're Freedom's Pioneers.

CHORUS.
O, slaves may beg, and cowards whine;
    We scorn their foolish fears.
We dare and plan to lead the van,
    With Freedom's Pioneers.

Too long upon our toil were built
    The palaces of power,
When at our word those forts of guilt
    Would crumble in an hour;
Now each day brings on swiftest wings
    To their unwilling ears,
The shouts that greet our marching feet,
    " 'Tis Freedom's Pioneers."

8

The rich man's hate, the rich man's pride
    Hath held us long in awe,
Our Right to Life is still denied,
    And wealth still rules the law.
But man shall bow no longer now,
    But welcomes with his cheers
The ringing stroke to break his yoke
    Of Freedom's Pioneers.

(Chorus.)

JAMES CONNOLLY.

DRINKING AND THINKING.

(The Irish words "Cruiscin Lan" signify in English, "Full Pitcher," and are pronounced as written in the more commonly known vulgarized English version to the same tune.—Ed.)

Air—"Cruiskeen Lawn."

Let the farmers praise their grounds,
    And sportsmen praise their hounds,
And shepherds their dew-scented lawn,
    But we, more blithe than they,
    Spend each happy night and day,
O'er our smiling little Cruiscin Lan.

Let doctors praise their health,
    And misers praise their wealth,
Repent, cries the prelate in lawn,
    But if the whole were hanged,
    We'll not part while we can stand,
From our smiling little Cruiscin Lan.

The mighty Thomas Paine,
    Who Freedom did maintain
With energy of reason and of sense,
    Was as stupid as an ass,
    Till first he took a glass,
Then truth sprang from his Cruiscin Lan.

The patriotic French
    Before they advanced an inch
Against the detested Bastile,
    Had filled each cup and can
    To the glorious rights of man,
And they quaffed them off in Cruiscin Lan.

Then fill your glasses high,
    Let's not part with lips so dry,
Though the lark should proclaim the new dawn,
    Since here we can't remain,
    May we shortly meet again
To take another Cruiscin Lan.

IRELAND, 1798.

9

A LOVE SONG.

Tune—"Believe Me if All Those Endearing
Young Charms."

I love you, I love you, tho' toil may obscure
And make darker the light of my eye,
Tho' slow runs my blood, and my heart, if as
pure,
Beats calmer when women are nigh;
Yet out from my heart comes a passionate wail,
With a note of sincerity true,
The protest of that heart, tho' its vigor may
fail,
Yet beats stronger its love, dear, for you.

I love you, I love you, no swain to his dear,
Nor mother to first fruit of her womb,
Nor thinker to truths he has garnered in tears
From the deserts which hid them in gloom,
Hath love more devoted, more unfailing than
he,
Now laying this poor wreath at thy shrine,
In the hope that accepted that offering will be,
And remembered when victory is thine.

Yes, Freedom, I love you, my soul thou hast
fired
With the flame that redeems from the clay,
Thou hast given to me, as to Moses inspired,
A glimpse of that land bright as day,
Whither Labor must journey, tho' each foot of
the road
Sweated blood from the graves of its best,
Where, built upon justice and truth, the abode
Thou preparest awaits the opprest.

                              JAMES CONNOLLY.

FREEDOM OF LABOR.

Tune—"McGregor's Gathering."
"THE MARCH OF THE CAMERON MEN"
Fill your glasses once more, fill them up to the
brim
And drink a last toast ere we part,
For here's to the triumph, now well on its way,
Of the cause that lies nearest our heart,
Drink it long, drink it deep, 'tis the toast of the
brave,
And lustily swell the refrain,
Here's death to the system of master and slave,
And "The Freedom of Labor" again.
                    And again, yet again,
            'Tis the Freedom of Labor again.

10

Ah, comrades, the men who toil and in gloom
  Hewed the path that we tread on to-day,
Our rulers ordained us to kill them and we
  Knew only to bow and obey.
And deep was our sin, yet repentance at last
  Shall weaken and wash out the stain,
And repentance means tryanny, tramled,
    downcast,
  And the Freedom of Labor again,
      And again, yet again,
    Tis the Freedom of Labor again.

Ah, God, how the tyrants laughed loud in their
    glee,
  As we swore to them true to abide,
And slaughtered each other all over the earth,
  To pamper their power and their pride,
And priests sang hosannas in praise of their
    might,
  And worshipped their rule and their reign,
But hurrah for the thinking that brought us the
    light,
  And the Freedom of Labor again,
      And again, yet again,
    'Tis the Freedom of Labor again.

Fill your glasses once more, fill them up to the
    brim,
  Let your cheers ring applause to the toast,
How the future will envy the name and the
    fame
  Of the man who can honor it most.
To your feet! Here's the cause that can never
    be lost
  While burns a thought in the brain,
Here's the men who died for it, ne'er counting
    the cost,
Here's the Freedom of Labor again,
      And again, yet again,
    'Tis the Freedom of Labor again,
                    JOHN LESLIE.

HUMAN FREEDOM.

Air—"Clare's Dragoons."

Scotch Air—"Happy We've Ben A' Thegither."
  Come, hearken all, the day draws nigh,
  When mustering hosts the cause shall try,
  Of Labour's right to live and die
              Enjoying human freedom;

22

11

Then Labour's force shall take the field,
The liberating sword to wield,
For Labour's own right arm must shield
        The cause of human freedom.

        Chorus.
Shout hurra, for freedom's host,
  For freedom's banner nobly borne,
Shout hurra, though tempest tossed,
  Freedom's barque shall ride the storm.

The rights our heroes lives have bought,
The truths our martyrs, dying, taught,
The hearts of men with passion hot.
        Prepare for human freedom;

Its roots are in no barren soil,
But watered by the tears of toil,
Are spreading fast, no storms can spoil
        The plant of human freedom.

Our Native Land, alas, the name,
Is but a sound to tell our shame,
What land have they whose spirits tame
        Brook loss of human freedom.

When lake and river, hill and dale,
Hear children's cry and women's wail
Of suffering rise on every gale,
        For lack of human freedom.

Our banner waves o'er many bands
Thro' mount and ocean-severed lands,
With active brain and skilful hands
        Working for human freedom;

For ancient feuds no more divide,
And ancient hates we thrust aside,
Our class, we know, thro' battle's tide
        Must bear the flag of freedom.

For this, since ere the world began,
Their troubled course the ages ran,
And earth, in long travail for man,
        Bare seed of human freedom;

For us and ours that heritage
Was handed down from age to age,
That we might write on Hist'ry's page—
        The Birth of Human Freedom.

Shout hurra, for freedom's host,
  For freedom's banner nobly borne,
Shout hurra, though tempest tossed,
  Freedom's barque shall ride the storm.
           JAMES CONNOLLY.

12

THE RED FLAG.

(By James Connell, an Irish writer, long prominent in the Socialist movement of England.)

Tune—"The White Cockade" or "Tannenbaum."

The people's flag is deepest red,
  It shouded oft our martyred dead,
And e'er their limbs grew stiff and cold
  Their hearts' blood dyed its every fold.

Chorus.
Then raise the scarlet standard high,
  Beneath its folds we'll live and die,
Tho' cowards flinch and traitors sneer,
  We'll keep the red flag flying here.

Look round, the Frenchman loves its blaze,
  The sturdy German chants its praise,
In Moscow's vaults its hymns are sung,
  Chicago swells its surging song.

It waved above our infant might,
  When all ahead seemed dark as night,
It witnessed many a deed and vow;
  We will not change its colors now.

With heads uncovered swear we all
  To bear it onward till we fall,
Come dungeons dark or gallows grim,
  This song shall be our parting hymn.

It suits to-day the meek and base,
  Whose minds are fixed on pelf and place,
To cringe beneath the rich man's frown,
  And haul that sacred emblem down.

FOR LABOR'S RIGHT.

Translation of the famous revolutionary song "Auf Social-
isten" sung in chorus by the German Socialists at the close
of the Stuttgart Congress.

Up, brothers, up the drums are beating,
  And see on high the banners wave,
Close up our ranks, let no retreating
  Be ours whilst earth contains a slave.
    'Till all alike our triumph won
    Shall know the splendor of the sun,
    And drink of wisdom's holiest spring,
    This is the prize our armies bring.
      Chorus.
    A holy war for Labor's right,
    A holy war for Labor's right;
      For Labor's cause,
      For Labor's cause
    Shall win the fight.

24

13

O, brothers, ye whose hearts uncounted
  Must toil to win a scanty wage,
Whose backs were bent that robbers, mounted,
  Might ride thereon from age to age.
No longer now in thraldom grown,
Your strong right hand must take your own
And by that act to manhood spring
Such is the prize our armies bring.

Chorus.

The tyrants hope a conquering sword
  Will stem the onward march of right,
But Truth o'er all their barbarous horde
  Leads Freedom's host to Freedom's height.
To break the sword of war and pain
That peace and joy o'er earth may reign
And conquering hosts of Labor sing
This is the prize our armies bring.

JAMES CONNOLLY.

LIFT THE FLAG.

Tune "The Legacy."

Lift that flag and tenderly guard it,
  Guard it as lover would guard his love,
Ours be the shame if ought debarred it
  Freely floating our ranks above,
Grasp that flag, and proudly daring
  All that the tyrant can do or essay,
Strike, and the fetters they long are wearing
  From the limbs of Labor shall fall away.

Hail that flag, my brothers, 'tis ours,
  Ours the life-blood that gave it its hue,
For us it waved thro' darkest hours
  Waiting 'till Labor its destiny knew.
See that flag, now floating on high,
  Free as the eagle flies to the sun
Token and sign tho' men may die
  The cause persists whilst blood doth run.

Pledge that flag; my brothers, your glasses
  Never were drained to a holier toast;
Never shall Time reveal as it passes
  A grander mission than Labor can boast,
Fill up your glass! no stinted measure
  Shall serve to pledge this day with me,
The Cause we love, the Hope we treasure
  The Flag that beckons to Liberty.

JAMES CONNOLLY.

14

THE MARSEILLAISE.

(Translation by Richard Brinsley Sheridan, of the
famous Anthem of revolutionary France. On
the march of the Northern Insurgents to
Antrim, Ireland, in 1798, Jamie Hope sung
this song, and all his comrades swelled the
chorus.)

Ye sons of France, awake to glory,
   Hark, what myriads bid you rise.
Your children, wives, and grandsires hoary,
   Behold their tears, and hear their cries!
Shall hateful tyrants, mischief breeding,
     With hireling hosts, a ruffian band,
     Affright and desolate the land,
While Peace and liberty lie bleeding.
    To arms, to arms, ye brave,
    The avenging sword unsheathe,
March on, march on, all hearts resolved,
    On victory or death.

Now, now, the dangerous storm is rolling,
   Which treacherous kings, confederate, raise,
The dogs of war, let loose are howling,
   And lo! our towns and cities blaze.
And shall we basely view the ruins,
     While lawless force with guilty stride,
     Spreads desolation far and wide.
In crimes and blood, his hands imbruing,
    To arms, to arms, ye brave, etc.

With luxury and pride surrounded,
   The vile, insatiate, despots dare,
Their thirst of power and gold unbounded,
   To meet and vend the light and air,
Like beasts of burden would they load us,
     Like gods, would bid their slaves adore,
     But man is man, and who is more?
Then shall they longer lash and goad us.
    To arms, to arms, ye brave, etc.

O Liberty! can man resign thee?
   Once having felt thy generous flame,
Can dungeons, bolts, and bars confine thee,
   Or whips thy noble spirit tame?
Too long, the world hath wept, bewailing,
   That falsehood's dagger tyrants wield,
But Freedom is our sword and shield,
    And all their arts are unavailing.
    To arms, to arms, ye brave, etc.

15

A SOCIALIST WAR SONG.

Tune—"O'Donnell Abu."

Shout, for the rage of the wronged has ascended!
  Shout, for the tyrants no longer hold sway,
Shout, for the rule of the robbers is ended,
  Shout, for the vengeance before us to-day!
      They who ne'er pity knew
      Now will have cause to rue;
Hunger and hardships they made us to dree,
      Helots in hunger nursed,
      Slaves of their reign accursed,
Stint not your vengeance till Labour is free!

Fools as we were in their honor confiding,
  We furnished their feasts with the price of
      our shame,
And our meanness was food for their mirth and
      deriding;
  In murder they steeped us to blazon their
      fame!
      Now as with naked glaives
      Stand we no longer slaves,
Freemen to tyrants no debtors should be;
      Down on the hated foe,
      Pay back the debt we owe,
Coined in their carnage till Labour is free!

Joy for the day when our standard as omen
  And sign of salvation floats proudly on high,
When its grim ruddy glare in the sun tells the
      foemen
  Around it we've sworn to conquer or die!
      Strong in our countless might,
      Strong in our conscious right,
Down on their armies like waves of the sea,
      On, know not break nor pause,
      On, in your children's cause,
Strike home and spare not till Labour is free!

The slogan is sounding, hurrah, how it gathers
  The thousands from city, and mountain, and
      plain,
Who have vowed to be free in the land of their
      fathers,
  No more to submit to the yoke and the chain.
      Forward the red flag, then,
      On, now as valiant men,
Freedom looks on us and shouts her decree.
      Deep must our vengeance smart,
      Strike to the tyrant's heart,
Mercy we know not till Labour is Free!
                              —John Leslie.

16

FREEDOM'S SUN.

Air—"Love's Young Dream."

Yes, Freedom's song, by workers sung,
    Rings loud and clear,
O'er every land, in every tongue,
    Afar, anear;
    Time passeth by,
    Old systems die—
Oppression's course outrun,
But Earth, rejoiced, salutes the light
    Of Freedom's sun;
O, rejoicing Earth salutes the light
    Of Freedom's sun.

Yes, all men then their lives may live,
    From grim want free,
And all the joys that life can give,
    Their lot shall be;
    And care shall fly,
    And sea and sky
Acclaim the work well done,
When earth, rejoiced, salutes the light
    Of Freedom's sun;
O, rejoicing Earth salutes the light
    Of Freedom's sun.

No longer now revolt need hide
    in holes and caves,
While they who brave Oppression's pride,
    But find their graves.
    No tyrant's ban
    Can now make man
The truths of knowledge shun;
All Earth, rejoiced, salutes the light
    Of Freedom's sun;
O, rejoicing Earth salutes the light
    Of Freedom's sun.

Our fathers saw the master's sword
    His plunder glean,
But specious fraud and lying word
    His thefts now screen;
    Yet fraud shall fail
    And truth prevail,
And justice shall be done,
When Earth, rejoiced, salutes the light
    Of Freedom's sun;
O, rejoicing Earth salutes the light
    Of Freedom's sun.

JAMES CONNOLLY.

READY   DECEMBER 1, 1907

"The Harp"

Connolly

SOUVENIR

1919

Yours,
fighting and hoping,
James Connolly

Cumannact na hÉireann
42 North Great George's Street

Dublin

PRICE
6d.

Essential Truths

from Connolly . .

The Cause of Labour is the Cause of Ireland, the Cause of Ireland is the Cause of Labour. They cannot be dissevered. Ireland seeks Freedom. Labour seeks that an Ireland free should be the sole mistress of her own destiny, supreme owner of all material things within and upon her soil.

Labour seeks to make the Free Irish Nation the guardian of the interests of the people of Ireland, and to secure that end would vest in that Free Irish Nation all property rights as against the claims of the individual, with the end in view that the individual may be enriched by the nation, and not by the spoiling of his fellows.

* * *

We cannot conceive of a Free Ireland with a subject Working Class; we cannot conceive of a subject Ireland with a Free Working Class.

But we can conceive of a Free Ireland with a Working Class guaranteed the power of freely and peacefully working out its own salvation.

* * *

The Security of the People of Ireland has the same roots as the Security of the Irish Working Class. In the closely linked modern world no nation can be free which can nationally connive at the enslavement of any section of that nation.

* * *

Ireland has, for seven centuries, struggled in the grasp of England. For seven hundred years Ireland has seen–no generation which did not attempt insurrection aiming at driving the English power out of Ireland—for seven hundred years, with the exception of one brief period in the 18th century. during which religious persecution strangled every thought of national regeneration. This conquest of Ireland, and the battle for the re-conquest has ebbed and flowed, but has never ceased. England insisted that her very life demanded that Ireland should be stripped of all the essentials of true nationhood, that it was not possible that Ireland could be mistress of her own destiny and England live. Therefore that England might remain an Empire Ireland must remain a subject nation. From this standpoint England has not to this day receded one-millionth part of an inch.

* * *

The power which holds in subjection more of the world's population than any other power on the globe, and holds them in subjection as slaves without any guarantee of freedom or power of self-government, this power that sets Catholic against Protestant, the Hindoo against the Mohammedan, the Yellow man against the Brown, and keeps them quarrelling with each other whilst she robs and murders them all—this power appeals to Ireland to send her sons to fight under England's battle for the cause of the oppressed.

* * *

In the name of liberty it hangs and imprisons patriots, and whilst calling High Heaven to witness its horror of militarism it sends the shadow of its swords between countless millions and their hopes of Freedom.

* * *

The moment the worker no longer believes in the all-conquering strength of the employer is the moment when the way opens out to the emancipation of our class.

The master class realise this, and hence all their agencies bend their energies towards drugging, stupefying, and poisoning the minds of the workers—sowing distrust and fear amongst them.

* * *

Men and women are at all times zealous for honour, for the esteem of their fellows, and when the hope of plunder is removed out of the field of human possibility those specially gifted ones who now exhaust their genius in an effort to rule, will as vehemently exert themselves to win the honour accorded to those who serve.

James Connolly Birthday Celebration.

✦✦✦

MANSION HOUSE, DUBLIN.   THURSDAY, JUNE 5th, 1919.

Tickets—ONE SHILLING.   Proceeds to be devoted to the establishment of a
CONNOLLY MEMORIAL WORKERS' COLLEGE.

COMMITTEE:

CHAIRMAN: Mr. WILLIAM O'BRIEN.

TREASURER: **Mr. M. O'LEARY.**   SECRETARY: **Mr. GEO. SPAIN.**

Mrs. James Connolly.	Madame Gonne MacBride.
Miss Nora Connolly.	Mrs. Mallin.
Mr. R. Connolly.	Mr.. Joseph MacDonnell.
Mrs. Tom Clarke.	Mr. Sean McLoughlin.
Mrs. Cogley.	Mr. Tom Nagle.
Mr. Creagh.	Miss O'Brien.
Mr. M. Donnelly.	Mr. D. O'Leary.
Mr. Darrel Figgis.	Mr. Cathal O'Shannon.
Mr. Thos. Foran.	Mrs. Partridge.
Mr. Gerald Griffin.	Mr. Conrad Peterson.
Mr. J. J. Hughes.	Mr. Frank Robins.
Miss B. Kelly.	Mr. Eamonn Rooney.
Mr. Tom Kennedy.	Mrs. Sheehy Skeffington.
Mr. C. Kenny.	Miss M. Skinnider.
Mr. Walter Carpenter.	Mr. Jas. Smith.
Mr. Cogley.	Mr. Peter Spain.
Mr. Michael Judge.	Mr. H. Yeates.
Mrs. M. K. Connery.	Mr. J. Tuohy.
Doctor Kathleen Lynn.	Miss R. Timmon.
Madame Markievicz, T.D.E.	Miss L. Yeates.

...   Accompanist   ..   Miss MOLLY YEATES.

ART SOUVENIR PROGRAMME.   Price SIXPENCE.

JAMES CONNOLLY was born near Clones, Co. Monaghan, on June 5th, 1870, and spent his childhood in his Ulster home. Trained in the school of working-class life he learned to labour in the cold metropolis of the North (Edinburgh) at the early age of 11. In 1896 he returned to Ireland settling in Dublin with the avowed object of propagating Socialism. He took his part in Trade Union organisation and public life, in which even at twenty-six he was no novice, having been a Socialist Municipal candidate in the City of Edinburgh. After his arrival in Dublin he founded the Irish Socialist Republican Party.

In August 1898 he issued the first number of the "Workers' Republic." Wood Quay Ward rejected his candidature for Municipal honours in 1902 and 1903. In the latter year he emigrated to America where he helped to build up the Industrial Workers of the World, and founded the Irish Socialist Republican Federation, of whose organ, "The Harp," he became Editor.

The call of Erin drew him back in 1910.

From that date his activities and sacrifices, thought and writings became the warp and woof of Ireland's story during the building of the Transport Union, and its gigantic struggles for the rights of man. Located first in Belfast he came later to Dublin to share the burden of the great lock-out.

He had, ere this, at the Clonmel Congress, 1912, converted the Trade Union Congress to a recognition of Labour's need for independent political action. The Citizen Army, the Red Guard of the workers, formed in 1913, later made him Commandant, with Michael Mallin as Chief of Staff. The outbreak of war found him ready to combat militarism intellectually in the press at home, in the Glasgow "Forward," and in the "International Socialist Review" of Chicago; and physically in any chance that offered.

Of the last sacrifice we need not speak here, but it is well that in our gratitude for the oblation on the Altar of Liberty we should not forget that his life, like his death, was a perpetual offering of a man's worth and work on behalf of the common weal.

(1)

2

(3)

PROGRAMME

JAMES CONNOLLY BIRTHDAY CELEBRATION.

Mansion House, Dublin, 5th June, 1919, at 8 p.m.

1. CHAIRMAN'S ADDRESS ... ... Mr. WILLIAM O'BRIEN.
2. SONG ... ... "A Rebel Song."

MRS. FAY SARGENT

(5)

SONGS
OF THE WORKERS' REPUBLIC.

A REBEL SONG.
Words by JAMES CONNOLLY   Key G.   With Spirit
Music by G. W. Crawford, Edinburgh.

1 Come, wor-kers, sing a reb-el song, a song of love and hate— Of love un - to the

low-ly and of hat - red to the great, The great who trod our fathers down, who

steal our children's bread, Whose hand of greed is stretched to rob the liv-ing and the dead.

Chorus. *ff* Tempo

Then sing our reb - el song, as we proudly sweep a - long, To end the age - long

tyr-an - ny that makes for hu - man tears ; Our march is nearer done with each

set - ting of the sun, And the tyrant's might is passing with the passing of the years.

2 We sing no song of wailing, and no song of sighs or tears,
High are our hopes, and stout our hearts, and banished all our fears,
Our flag is raised above us so that all the world may see,
'Tis Labour's faith and Labour's arm alone can Labour free.

3 Out from the depths of misery we march with hearts aflame,
With wrath against the rulers false who wreck our manhood's name ;
The serf who licks his tyrant's rod may bend forgiving knee,
The slave who breaks his slavery's chain a wrathful man must be.

4 Our army marches onward with its face towards the dawn,
In trust secure in that one thing the slave may lean upon ;
The might within the arm of him who, knowing Freedom's worth,
Strikes home to banish tyranny from off the face of earth.

(6)

Programme—*continued*

3. SONG ... ... "The Watchword of Labour."

MR. FRANK ROBBINS.

4. ORATION. ... ... "James Connolly—Educationalist."

MR. CATHAL O'SHANNON.

5. VIOLIN and PIANO ... ... ("The Soul of Ireland." ... ... ("The Music of the People."

"CASEY" (Violin) and "DOLLY" (Piano).

(7)

THE WATCHWORD OF LABOUR.

JAMES CONNOLLY.   J. J. HUGHES.

Key F.   With Spirit.

Oh hear ye the watchword of La —   bour ! The slo — gan of they who'd be

free   That no more to an — y en - sla —   ver Must

lab - our bend sup-pliant knee   That we on whose shoul-ders are

bo —   rne, The pomp and the pride of the great ;   Whose

toil they re-pay with their sc — orn, Must chal-lenge and master our

Chorus

fate   Then send it al - oft   on the breeze   boys ! That

watch-word the grandest we've known,   That La-bour must rise from its

kn - ees boys ! And claim the broad earth as its own.

Aye ! we who oft won by our valour,
  Empire for our Rulers and Lords,
Yet knelt in abasement and squalor,
  To the thing we had made by our
      swords.
Now valour with worth will be blending,
  When answering Labour's command,
We arise from our knees, and ascending
  To manhood for freedom take stand.

CHORUS.—Then send it aloft, etc.

Then out from the field and the city,
  From workshop, from mill, and from
      mine,
Despising their wrath and their pity,
  We workers are moving in line,
To answer the watchword and token,
  That Labour gives forth as its own ;
Nor pause till our fetters we've broken,
  And conquered the spoiler and drone.

CHORUS.—Then send it aloft, etc.

(8)

Programme—*continued.*

During the evening " Casey " will play items from the following :—

A Harp Lament ; The Famine Song ; Song of an Island Fisherman ; Darby O'Dun ; Rinnce Fada ; Cuchullin's Lament ; The Coulin ; Paddies Evermore ; The Blackbird ; Harp that once ; The Plough Whistle ; Derry Love Song ; Castle of Dromore ; Patrick's Day ; Arranmore Boat Song ; Boat Song from the " Tales of Hoffman " ; Three Ave Marias—Gounod, Schubert, and Mascagni ; Andante Finale, Mendelssohn ; Romance, Beethoven ; Gipsy Dances ; Bird Song ; Devil's Sonata ; Selections from " Il Trovatore " ; Goblin Dance ; Mendelssohn's Spring Song ; Serenade ; Carnival of Venice ; Hungarian Dances ; Folk Songs, etc.

DANCE ... ... HORNPIPE ... Misses Kelly and Shanahan

(9)

A DYING SOCIALIST TO HIS SON.

Come here my son, and for a time put up
  your childish play,
Draw nearer to your father's bed, and lay
  your games away,
No sick man's plaint is this of mine, ill-
  tempered at your noise,
Nor carping at your eagerness to romp with
  childish toys.
Thou'rt but a boy, and I, a man outworn
  with care and strife,
Would not deprive you of one joy thou
  canst extract from life;
But o'er my soul comes creeping on death's
  shadow, and my lips
Must give to you a message now ere life meets
  that eclipse.
Slow runs my blood, my nether limbs I feel
  not, and my eyes
Can scarce discern, here in this room, that
  childish form I prize.

Aye, death's grim hand is on my frame,
  and helpless it lies here,
But to my mental vision comes the power
  of the seer,
And time and space are now as nought as
  with majestic sweep,
I feel my mind traverse the land and encom-
  pass the deep;
Search backward over history's course, or
  with prophetic view
And sounding line of hope and fear, gauge
  man's great destiny, too.
The chasm deep 'twixt life and death, I
  bridge at last to-night,
And with a foot on either side absorb their
  truth and light,
And thus, my son, though reft of strength,
  my limbs slow turn to clay,
Fired by this light I call you here to hear
  my Legacy.

"My Legacy!" Ah, son of mine! Wert
  thou a rich man's pride,
He'd crown thee with his property, posses-
  sions far and wide,
And golden store to purchase slaves, whose
  aching brain and limb
Would toil to bring you luxury as such had
  toiled for him.
But thy father is a poor man, and glancing
  round you here,
Thou canst see all his property—our humble
  household gear,
No will we need by lawyers drawn, no wit-
  nesses attest,
To guard for you your legacy, your father's
  last bequest.

"Thy father is a poor man," mark well
  what that may mean,
On the tablets of thy memory that truth
  write bright and clean,
Thy father's lot it was to toil from earliest
  boyhood on,
And know his latent energies for a master's
  profit drawn;

Or else, ill-starred, to wander round and
  huxter-like to vend
His precious store of brain and brawn to
  all whom fate may send
Across his path with gold enough to purchase Labour's power,
To turn it into gold again, and fructify the
  hour
With sweat and blood of toiling slaves like
  unto us my son;
Aye, through our veins since earliest days,
  'tis poor man's blood has run.

Yes, son of mine, since History's dawn two
  classes stand revealed,
The Rich and Poor, in bitterest war, by
  deadliest hatred steeled,
The one, incarnate greed and crime disdain-
  ing honest toil,
Had grasped man's common birthright and
  treasure house, the soil.
And standing 'twixt their fellow men and
  all that earth could give,
Had bade them render tribute if they would
  hope to live.
And, building crime on top of crime, had
  pushed their conquests on,
Till, arbiters of life and death, they stood
  with weapons drawn
And blades athirst to drink the blood, on
  land and over sea,
Of him who dared for human rights to stem
  this tyranny.
They held our lands, our bodies ruled, and
  strove to rule the mind,
And Hell itself could not surpass their evil
  to mankind,
And all who strove for human rights to break
  their cursed yoke—
The noblest of our race, my child—went down
  beneath their stroke,
And over all earth's sweetest spots, in
  nature's loveliest haunt,
Each built his fort or castle grim the poor
  of earth to daunt.

And issuing forth from walls of stone, high
  over cliff and pass,
With sword in hand would gather in the
  tribute for his class.
And grimmest emblems of their rule flaunting
  to human ken,
The pit to drown our women, the gibbet
  for our men,
Stood, aye, beside their fortresses; and under-
  neath the moat
Tier under tier of noisome cells for those
  the tyrant smote.
Thumbscrew and rack and branding rod, and
  each device of Hell
Perverted genius could devise to torture men
  to sell
(For brief respite from anguish dire to end
  their wretched lives)
The secrets of their comradeship, the honour
  of their wives.

ᴸEGACY ✿ ✿ ✿

By JAMES CONNOLLY.

As fabled as the tree of old, by ancient poets
   sung,
Consumed with blight each living thing that
   'neath its branches sprung;
The rich man's power o'er all the earth had
   spread its baleful blight,
Respecting neither age nor sex to sate its
   lust for might.
It stole the harvest from the field, the pro-
   duct from the loom,
Struck down the old man in his age, the
   young man in his bloom,
It robbed the carrier on the road, the sailor
   on the tide,
And from the bridegroom of an hour it took
   the new-made bride.
Such crimes it wrought—not Hell itself and
   its Satanic school
Could fashion crimes to equal those wrought
   by the rich man's rule.
" The past ? " Ah, boy, the method's past ;
   the deed is still the same,
And robbery is robbery yet, though cloaked
   in gentler name.
Our means of life are still usurped, the rich
   man still is lord,
And prayers and cries for justice still meet
   one reply—the sword !
Though hypocrites for rich men's gold may
   tell us we are free,
And oft extol in speech and print our
   vaunted liberty.
But freedom lies not in a name, and he
   who lacks for bread,
Must have that bread tho' he should give
   his soul for it instead.
And we, who live by Labour, know that
   while they rule we must
Sell Freedom, brain, and limb, to win for us
   and ours a crust.

The robbers made our fathers slaves, then
   chained them to the soil,
For a little longer chain—a wage—we must
   exchange our toil.
But open force gives way to fraud, and force
   again behind
Prepares to strike if fraud should fail to keep
   man deaf and blind.
Our mothers see their children's limbs they
   fondled as they grew,
And doted on, caught up to make for rich
   men profits new.
Whilst strong men die for lack of work, and
   cries of misery swell,
And women's souls in cities' streets creep
   shuddering to hell.
These things belong not to the past, but to
   the present day,
And they shall last till in our wrath we sweep
   them all away.

"We sweep them !" Ah, too, well I know
   my work on earth is done,
E'en as I speak my chilling blood tells me
   my race is run.

But you, my last born child, take now the
   legacy I give,
And do as did your father whilst he yet was
   spared to live.
Treasure ye in your inmost heart this legacy
   of hate,
For those who on the poor man's back have
   climbed to high estate,
The lords of land and capital, the slave lords
   of our age,
Who of this smiling earth of ours have made
   for us a cage.
Where golden bars fetter men's souls, and
   noble thoughts do flame
To burn us with their vain desires, and virtue
   yields to shame.
Each is your foe, foe of your class, of human
   rights, the foe,
Be it your thought by day and night to work
   their overthrow ;
And howsoe'er you earn your wage, and
   wheresoe'er you go,
Be it beneath the tropic heat or mid the
   northern snow,
Or closely pent in factory walls or burrowing
   in the mine,
Or scorching in the furnace hell of steamers
   'cross the brine,
Or on the railroad's shining track you guide
   the flying wheel,
Or clambering up on buildings high to weld
   their frames of steel,
Or use the needle or the type, the hammer
   or the pen,
Have you one thought, one speech alone to
   all your fellow-men.
The men and women of your class, tell them
   their wrongs and yours—
Plant in their hearts that hatred deep that
   suffers and endures,
And treasuring up each deed of wrong, each
   scornful word and look,
Inscribe it in the memory, as others in a book.
And wait and watch through toiling years the
   ripening of time,
Yet deem to strike before that hour were
   worse than folly—crime.

This be your task, oh, son of mine, the rich
   man's hate to brave,
And consecrate your noblest part to rouse
   each fellow-slave
To speed the day the world awaits when
   Labour long opprest
Shall rise and strike for Freedom true, and
   from the tyrant's wrest
The power they have abused so long. Oh,
   ever-glorious deed !
The crowning point of history, yet, child, of
   bitterest need.

*   *   *   *   *

Ah, woe is me, thy father's eyes shall not
   behold that day.
I faint and die : child, hold my hand—
Keep—thou—my—Leg-a-cy !

43

Cumann ban-Oibre Éireann.

Irish Women Workers' Union

Head Office—DENMARK HOUSE,
21 GREAT DENMARK ST., DUBLIN

TWO years ago the women workers of Ireland were sweated, exploited, downtrodden. To-day the power of the Irish Women Workers' Union enables them to win not only

A FAIR LIVING WAGE,

BUT also to help in Labour's common struggle for the right of the workers to share in all the opportunities life offers for happiness, knowledge, adventure, enterprise, and acquaintance with Nature, Art, Science and Literature.

The Emancipation of the Workers is close at hand.

Women of Ireland unite to make it a noble Emancipation, faithful to the best conceptions of Liberty and Fraternity.

AFFILIATED ORGANIZATIONS:

Irish Nurses' Union, 29 South Anne Street, Dublin (the first Nurses' Union in Great Britain or Ireland). **Domestic Workers' Union, Denmark House.**

FOR LABOUR'S RIGHT.

JAMES CONNOLLY.   J. J. HUGHES.

Key F.

```
:.s₁ | d :-.s₁ | d :-.m | r : d | m.s: s | l : s | f : m |
```
Up broth - ers up! The drums are beat-ing, And see on High the

```
| r : d | s :.s₁ | d :-.s₁ | d :-.r | m : r | m.s: .s |
```
ban - ners wave, Close up your ranks, let no re - treating Be

```
| fe :-.m | r.m:fe.s | l : r | s :-.s | f : m | r : l |
```
ours while earth con - tains a slave; Till all a - like our

```
| s :-.f | m :.s | f : m | r : d | t₁'﹕d | r :.s₁ |
```
tri - umph won be- hold the splen-dour of the sun, and

```
| s₁ :-.d | m.r:d.t₁ | l₁ : r | f :m.f | s : d | l : f |
```
drink of wis - dom's hol - iest spring, This is the prize our

Chorus.

```
| m :-.r | d :.s₁ | s₁ :-.d | m.r:d.t₁ | l₁ :-.se₁ | l₁ :.l₁ |
```
arm - ies bring, A ho - ly war for La - bour's right, a

```
| r :-.m | f.m:r.d | t₁ : s | s : s₁ | s₁ :-.d | m.r:d.t₁ |
```
ho - ly war for Lab - our's right, For La - bour's cause, for

```
| l₁ : r | f :m.f | s : - | - :l.f | m : - | r :-.d |
```
La - bour's cause, shall win shall win ——— the

```
| d : - | - : ||
```
fight.

O. brothers, we whose hosts uncounted
  Must toil to earn a scanty wage;
Whose backs were bent that robbers
    mounted
  Might ride thereon from age to age.
No longer now in thraldom grown
Your strong right hand must take your
    own;
And by that act to manhood spring!
This is the prize our armies bring!
        Chorus.

The tyrant hopes a conquering sword
Shall stem the onward march of right
But truth o'er all their barbarous horde
  Leads Freedom's host to Freedom's
    height!
To break the sword of War and Pain
That Peace and Joy o'er Earth may reign
And conquering hosts of Labour sing—
This is the prize our armies bring!

        Chorus.

(4

WORKS OF
JAMES CONNOLLY

Author of

1897. Erin's Hope.
1898. New Evangel.
1908- Socialism Made Easy.
1910. Labour Nationality and Religion.
1910. Labour in Irish History
1914. Re-Conquest of Ireland

Editor of

1896. Rights of Ireland and the Faith of a Felon (LALOR)
1897. '98 Readings
1898. "Workers' Republic"
1908. "The Harp," U.S.A.
1914. "The Irish Worker"
1915. "The Worker"
1915. "The Workers' Republic"

Numerous Contributions to

An ⁊Sean Bean Bocꞇ, "Labour Leader," "Socialist," "Forward," "New Age," "International Socialist Review," "Irish Review," "Irish Nation," and many American Socialist Journals.

(15)

THE CALL OF ERIN.

JAMES CONNOLLY.　　　　　Air " Rolling Home to Bonnie Scotland."

Key C.

|:d . m | s :-.s:fe,s | l.s :— :m.s | m¹. :-.d¹:s.m |

With the　en - gines neath us throb-bing,　and the wind　up - on our

| r : — :t.d¹ | r¹ :-.d¹:t.f | l.s : — :fe.s |

stern,　Lit-tle reck　we of the　dis tance　that div-

| t :-.l:f.s | m : — :d.m | s :-.s:fe.s |

ides　us now from Erin　For we　hear　her voices

| l.s : — :m.s | m¹ :-.d¹:s.m | r : — :t.d¹ |

call-ing　Sweep-ing past　us on the　west　Call-ing

| r¹ :-.d¹:t.f | l.s : — :fe.s | t :-.l:f.r |

home　to her the child-ren　She once　nour -ished on her

Chorus.

| d : — :d.m | s :-.s:fe.s | l.s : — :m.s |

breast.　She is　call -ing, call-ing, call-ing　in the

| m¹ :-.d¹:s.m | r : — :t.d¹ | r¹ :-.d¹:t.f |

wind　and o'er the tide　We, her　child - ren hear her

| l.s : — :fe.s | t :-.l:f.r | d : — : ‖ |

voices　call us　ev - er to her side.

Oh ! ye waters bear us onward
　And ye winds your task fulfil,
Till our Irish eyes we feast on
　Irish vale and Irish hill ;
Till we tread our Irish Cities,
　See their glory and their shame
And our eyes like skies o'er Erin,
　Through their smiles shed tears of pain.

Glorious is the land we're leaving
　And its pride shall grow through years
And the land that calls us homewards
　Can but share with us her tears :
Yet our heart her call obeying,
　Heedless of the wealth men crave,
Turneth home to share her sorrow,
　Where she weeps beside the wave.

CHORUS.　　　　　　　　　　CHORUS.

(16)

Programme—*continued.*

9. SONG. ... ... "The Call of Erin."

   MR. SEAN ROGAN.

10. PART SONG. ... ... "The International."

   S. P. I CHOIR.

11. FINALE. ... ... "The Red Flag."

   MR. A. BRASIL.

(17)

THE INTERNATIONAL.

(E. POTTIER.)

———

Arise ye starvlings from your slumbers,
  Arise ye criminals of want,
For reason in revolt now thunders,
  And at last ends the age of cant.
Now away with all superstitions,
  Servile masses, Arise! Arise!
We'll change forthwith the old conditions,
  And spurn the dust to win the prize.

CHORUS

  Then comrades, come rally, the last fight let
    us face—
  L'Internationale unites the human race.
  Then comrades, come rally, the last fight
    let us face—
  L'Internationale unites the human race.

We're tricked by laws and regulations,
  Our taxes strip us to the bone,
The rich enjoy the wealth of nations;
  But the poor naught can call their own.
Long have we in vile bondage languished,
  Yet we equal are every one;
No rights but duties for the vanquished,
  We claim our rights for duties done.

              CHORUS.

The kings defile us with their powder;
  We want no war within the land,
Let soldiers strike; for peace call louder,
  Lay down arms and join hand in hand.
Should these vile monsters still determine,
  Heroes to make us in despite.
They'll know full soon the kind of vermin
  Our bullets hit in this last fight.

              CHORUS.

The kings of mines, and ships, and railways,
  Resplendent in their vulgar pride,
Have plied their task to exploit always
  Those who labour they've e'er decried.
Great the spoil they hold in their coffers,
  To be spent on themselves alone;
We'll seize it some day, spite of scoffers,
  And feel that we have got our own.

              CHORUS.

We peasants, artisans, and soldiers,
  Enrolled among the sons of toil,
Let's claim the earth henceforth for brothers,
  Drive the indoleut from the soil.
On our flesh long has fed the raven,
  We've too long been the vultures prey;
But now, farewell this spirit craven;
  The dawn brings in a brighter day.

              CHORUS.

THE RED FLAG.

(JIM CONNELL.)

The people's flag is deepest red,
  It shrouded oft our martyred dead;
And ere their limbs grew stiff and cold,
  Their hearts blood dyed its every fold.

Chorus.

Then raise the scarlet standard high,
  Within its shade we'll live and die;
Though cowards flinch and traitors sneer,
  We'll keep the Red Flag flying here.

Look round! The Frenchman loves its blaze
  The sturdy German chants its praise;
In Moscow's halls its hymns are sung,
  Chicago swells the surging throng.

    CHORUS —Then raise etc.

It waved above our infant might,
  When all ahead seemed dark as night;
It witnessed many a deed and vow,
  We must not change its colour now.

    CHORUS.—Then raise, etc.

It well recalls the triumphs past,
  It gives the hope of peace at last;
The banner bright, the symbol plain,
  Of human right and human gain.

    CHORUS.—Then raise, etc.

It suits to-day the weak and base,
  Whose minds are fixed on pelf and place,
To cringe before the rich man's frown,
  And haul the sacred emblem down.

    CHORUS.—But raise, etc.

With heads uncovered swear we all,
  To bear it onward till we fall,
Come dungeon dark or gallows grim,
  This song shall be our parting hymn.

    CHORUS —Oh raise, etc.

18

THE STOREHOUSE OF KNOWLEDGE

The books and pamphlets catalogued below can be purchased at 42
North Great George's Street, Dublin, any evening from 8 p.m., or
:: :: :: :: may be ordered by post. :: :: :: ::

NORA CONNOLLY, writing in the "Voice of Labour," about her father, said :—
"Always he studied revolution. Every book dealing with revolution, social or
otherwise, was read and studied by him in the hope of gleaning some plan or
method that would assist him in his preparation for the Social Revolution."

RODERIC CONNOLLY in the same issue of the "Voice" said :—"To become
competent to achieve and maintain their Revolution, the Irish workers will be
assisted almost wholly in their task by an earnest study of the second part of
'Socialism Made Easy,' by James Connolly, where the broad principles of the
Dictatorship may be gleaned ; and by learning how Connolly's friends applied these
in a country so like Ireland as Russia, as detailed in Trotsky's 'History of the
Russian Revolution.' "

Economic Discontent. FATHER HEGARTY.
(Post free 2½d.) 2d
Wage, Labour and Capital. KARL MAX.
(Post free 2½d.) 2d
Value. Price and Profit. KARL MARX. (Post
free 4½d.) 4d
Marx and Modern Capitalism. NEWBOLD.
(Post free 2½d.) 2d
Politics of Capitalism. NEWBOLD. (Post
free 2½d.) 2d
Evolution of Industry. McLAINE. (Post
free 3½d.) 3d
Strength of the Strong. JACK LONDON.
(Post free 5½d.) 5d

Karl Marx : His Life and Teaching. ZELDA
KAHAN-COATES. (Post free 2½d.) ... 2d
Socialism and Individual Liberty. FRANK
TANNER. (Post free) 2½d.) ... 2d
Socialism and the Catholic Faith. BLAND
(Post free 2½d.) 2d
Evolution of Property. PAUL LAFARGUE.
(Post free 1/9) 1s. 6d
Through Dictatorship to Democracy.
KLARA ZETKIN. (Post free 3½d.) ... 3d
The German Spartacists : Spartacus Union
Declaration. (Post free 2½d.) ... 2d
Are You A Trade Unionist? LENIN AND
THEITCHERINE. (Post free 1½d.) ... 1d

A WORKERS LIBRARY ON BOLSHEVISM

The Soviets at Work. LENIN. (Post free
8d.) 6d
Collapse of The Second International.
LENIN. (Post free 1s. 2d.) ... 1s
The Bolshevik Revolution. LITVINOFF.
(Post free 9d.) 7d
The Chief Task of Our Times. LENIN. 3d
Questions and Answers about Russia.
W. S. F. 4d
Hands Off Russia : with large Map. WM
PAUL. 4d
British Consul's Replies to Slanders.
YOUNG. 3d
New Russia (with Constitution) ARNOLD.
3d

Internal Problems of Russia. ARNOLD. 3d
Hands Off Russia: A Speech. ZANGWILL
2d
Russian League of Nations Plan. W. S. F.
2d
Soviet Russia (Litvinoff), Gorki on the
Bolsheviks; Law Concerning Marriage;
each 1d
Present Struggle in Russia; Social Re-
construction; British Soldiers in Russia.
each ½d
History of Russian Revolution. L.
TROTSKY (Post free 2s. 9d.) ... 2s. 6d
Capitalist Russia and Socialist Russia
M. PHILIPS PRICE (Post free 4s. 2d.) 4s

FOUR WORKS ABOUT IRISH LABOUR

The Irish Labour Movement, RYAN. (Post
free 2s. 10d). ... ... 2s. 6d.
Ireland at Berne. OFFICIAL. (Post free
7d.) ... ... 6d.

Socialism Made Easy. CONNOLLY. Post
free 2½d.) 2d
Rebel Ireland W. S. F. (Post free 3½d.) 3d

Now in the Press, New Edition of JAMES CONNOLLY'S

LABOUR, NATIONALITY AND RELIGION

This famous Book, long out of print, recalls the great battle of intellect between the
eminent Jesuit, Father Robert Kane, and James Connolly. The new edition will be
the book of the moment. Book your order now by sending 9d. and 2d. for postage.

Order from Literature Secretary, Cumannaċt na héineann

42 NORTH GREAT GEORGE'S STREET, DUBLIN

20

The
James Connolly
Songbook

Published by :

THE CORK WORKERS CLUB

Price   -   -   -   -   -   15p

Contents
James Connolly Songbook (1972/1980)

Introduction to *The James Connolly Songbook*

> No revolutionary movement is complete without its po-
> etical expression. If such a movement has caught hold
> of the imagination of the masses, they will seek a vent in
> song for the aspirations, the fears and hopes, the loves
> and hatreds engendered by the struggle. Until the move-
> ment is marked by the joyous, defiant, singing of revo-
> lutionary songs, it lacks one of the distinctive marks of a
> popular revolutionary movement; it is a dogma of a few,
> and not the faith of the multitude.
>
> —James Connolly, Introduction,
> *Songs of Freedom*, N.Y., 1907

THIS LITTLE SONGBOOK is based on a selection of songs and recitation which were performed at a concert, given by James Connolly's comrades of the Socialist Party of Ireland and the Irish Citizen Army, to commemorate the anniversary of his birth. The concert was due to be held in the Mansion House, Dublin, on the 5th June, 1919, with members of the Citizen Army, described in the *Souvenir* programme as the "Red Guard of the workers," acting as stewards. However, British Imperialism, which had executed Connolly only three years previously, was intent on coercing those who would "seek a vent in song, for the aspirations, the fears and hopes, the loves and hatreds engendered by the struggle" and accordingly, the concert was proclaimed under the Defence of the Realm Act (D.O.R.A.). When the people arrived for the concert, they found the Mansion House guarded by armed police and many more police positioned in the nearby streets. Immediately, fully armed groups of the Citizen Army were mobilized. A Citizen Army officer who was trying to resist arrest fired on the police; his men followed his example and Dublin had its first shooting since Dan Breen and his comrades raised the standard at Soloheadbeg. Several policemen and one civilian were wounded. Later that night, the proclaimed concert was held in the Trades Hall. While the police and the "Red Guard of the workers" faced one another in the street outside, "the joyous, defiant singing of revolutionary songs" could be heard coming from the building. Among the songs that appeared on the programme were Connolly's rousing "Watchword of Labour" and "A Rebel Song." Meathman Jim Connell's "Red Flag," and the worker's anthem "The International." Many versions of several of these songs have been sung over the years. We are republishing them as they appeared on the *Souvenir* programme.

In addition to the songs on that memorable programme, we have included some of Connolly's lesser known recitations and "songs of freedom." The airs of his more popular songs are still well known among workers in Ireland. Many of Connolly's songs, like many working-class songs of the time, were sung to the air of popular songs, but, as many of these airs have long passed on in public memory, we suggest that where possible, workers should adapt his songs to the airs of today's popular songs and ballads. The music for *Watchword of Labour* was written by J.J. Hughes, a member of the S.P.I. and the music for *A Rebel Song* was by G.W. Crawford, of the Edinburgh Branch of the Socialist Labour Party.

EDITOR'S NOTE: The Cork Workers Club first published *The James Connolly Songbook* in 1972. The back cover of that edition announced the publication of *Ireland Upon the Dissecting Table: A Collection of James Connolly's Writings on Ulster and Partition*, collected and edited by the Cork Workers Club. Both the 1972 songbook and the collection of Connolly's writings about Ulster and Partition, are out of print. But those interested should search libraries and archives in Ireland, the UK, the United States, and other countries where copies were originally sent and are still likely to be found.

In 1980 the Cork Workers Club republished *The James Connolly Songbook*, as Number 5 in a series of twenty Historical Reprints. This edition comprised the same selection of songs and the same introduction as the 1972 version—and it was, incidentally, the 1980 version that I first discovered and used for Connolly's lyrics. However, one important difference between the two versions was that the back cover to the 1980 edition listed all twenty of the Historical Reprints, "of pamphlets, booklets and newspaper articles of historical value to the study of the Socialist Movement in Ireland." Two are of special interest in that they were collections of Connolly's writings organized by the Cork Workers Club to address conflicts raging in the 1970s and 1980s. The first of these was the aforementioned *Ireland Upon the Dissecting Table*, the second was *The Connolly–DeLeon Controversy: On Wages, Marriage and the Church*. Now, the 1980 version of *The James Connolly Songbook* can still be found in some bookstores or by internet search, as I was able to do in 2010. It is furthermore likely that diligent research will lead to finding, either online or in print form, all those publications in the Historical Reprints series. Certainly, it is worth the effort if one wishes to gain a better understanding of history and the crucial role James Connolly played in making it.

One further point needs to be added: the reproduction of the original *Songs of Freedom* and the 1919 program are exact facsimiles, necessary in order to make these crucial historical documents available to all. The reproduction of *The James Connolly Songbook* contains only those songs that did not appear in either of the other two songbooks since such repetition was unnecessary and it is still possible to find copies of the 1980 edition. It should nonetheless be kept in mind that the Cork Workers Club did in fact assemble, through painstaking effort, all the lyrics Connolly is known to have published, making *The James Connolly Songbook* the most comprehensive collection of Connolly's poetic writings yet available.

Arouse!

Arouse! The rallying cry
Sends its chorus up on high
Let craven cowards fly
    To the rear:
While we rally to fight
To our combat for the Right,
And Oppression put to flight,
    We swear.

For tyrants we have fought
And our blood (their gold had bought);
They have lavished, caring naught,
    In red streams
But the fight we have begun
On this earth shall ne'er be done
Till the light of Freedom's sun
    On us gleams.

At our lot might angels weep,
While we toil our masters sleep,
What we make out masters keep,
    And our gains,
Are the wage—to buy our food,
The poor shelter for our brood,
And the fever which our blood
    Ever drains.

By our toil they keep their state,
On our woes they rise, elate,
Yet wonder when our hate
    To them ascends;
Where we build they enter in,
What we earn those spoilers win
But we swear our slav'ry's sin
    Soon shall end.

Then arouse! ye workers all,
Braving scaffold, sword, and ball
And at Labour's trumpet call
    Quick appear,
For the day we long have sought,
For which out fathers fought—
The day with Freedom fraught
    Now is here!

"Be Moderate"
Air—*A Nation Once Again*

Some men, faint-hearted, ever seek
    Our programme to retouch,
And will insist, when'er they speak
    That we demand too much.
'Tis passing strange, yet I declare
    Such statements cause me mirth,
For our demands most modest are,
We only want THE EARTH.

"Be Moderate," the timorous cry,
    Who dread the tyrant's thunder,
"You ask too much, and people fly
    From you aghast, in wonder"
'Tis passing strange, and I declare
    Such statements cause me mirth,
For our demands most moderate are,
We only want THE EARTH.

Our masters all—a godly crew
    Whose hearts throb for the poor—
Their sympathies assure us, too,
    If our demands were fewer.
Most generous souls, but please observe,
    What they enjoy from birth,
Is all we ever had the nerve
    To ask, that is, THE EARTH.

The Labour Fakir, full of guile,
    Such doctrine ever preaches,
And, whilst he bleeds the rank and file,
    Tame moderation teaches.
Yet, in his despite, we'll see the day
    When, with sword in its girth,
Labour shall march in war array,
    To seize its own, THE EARTH.

For Labour long with groans and tears
    To its oppressors knelt.
But, never yet to aught save fears
    Did hear of tyrant melt.
We need not kneel; our cause is high,
    Of true men there's no dearth,
And our victorious rallying cry
    Shall be, WE WANT THE EARTH.

O Slaves of Toil!

When man shall stand erect at last,
    And drink at Wisdom's fountain,
And to the earth in scorn shall cast
    The chains his limbs are bound in;
Then from his loins a race shall spring,
    Fit peer of gods and heroes,
O, blest be they whose efforts bring
    That day and hour more near us.

CHORUS
O, Slaves of toil, no craven fear,
    Nor dread of fell disasters
Need daunt ye now, then up, and clear
    The earth of lords and masters.

Like brazen serpent raised on high,
    In Israelite tradition,
Our cause in each believing eye,
    Mean slavery's abolition,
We see the day when man shall rise,
    And, firm on science building,
From Theft's thick mask of fraud and lies
    Strip all the specious gilding.

CHORUS

O, blest are they whom wind and tide
    Are wafting fortune's graces,
And blest the man whose blushing bride
    Returns his rapt embraces,
And blest is he who has a friend
    To shield his name when slandered
But blest o'er all they who contend
    And march in Freedom's vanguard.

CHORUS

The Message
Air—*Sean O Duibhir an Ghleanna*

Our message send again
Pealing thro' hill and glen,
Freedom for working men
    Is freedom for all;
Freedom from dread of want,
From hunger, lean and gaunt,
From all the ills that daunt
    And keep us in thrall.

Up on the mountain side,
Far o'er the ocean tide,
Circling the world wide,
    That message is borne;
Bringing to those whose hearts
Ache 'neath the stings and darts.
Bondage to man imparts,
    Hope of Freedom's morn.

Morning when man shall rise
And face, with gladdened eyes,
The truth that Freedom lies
    In Labour's arms alone;
Labour, which makes to bloom
Mountain steppe and desert gloom,
Yet finds this life a tomb,
    And each hour a moan.

Moaning for manhood lost,
For noble purpose crossed,
For hopes and bright dreams tossed
    In that yawning grave,
Where wealth, the tyrant, stands,
Grasping with greedy hands,
And binding in iron bands,
    The life of its slave.

That message send again
Peeling thro' hill and glen,
Freedom for working men
    Is freedom for all;
Freedom from dread of want,
From hunger, lean and gaunt,
From all the ills that daunt
    And keep us in thrall.

The Blackleg

There's a cuckoo in our household,
And he terrifies our young,
For the habits of the traitor,
Have been often told and sung,
Though his feathers flutter softly,
There is murder in his heart,
And all down the toiling ages
He has played the villain's part.

Chorus
Oh, we hate the cruel tiger,
And hyena and jackal;
But the false and dirty blackleg
Is the vilest beast of all.

When we dress our brave battalions,
And confront the Lords of Loot,
We behold the Scab desert us
Ere the guns begin to shoot,
Just to gorge his greedy stomach,
And to save his coward skin,
With salvation in the balance
He betrays his kith and kin.

Chorus

You can tell him 'midst a thousand
By his cringe and by his crawl,
For of dignity or courage
He possesses none at all.
In the aleshop he's a sponger,
In the workshop he's a spy;
He's a liar and deceiver
With low cunning in his eye.

Chorus

Let us flout him in the market,
Let us "cut" him in the street,
Let us jeer him from all places
Where the honest workers meet,
When to his brazen features
Every decent door is slammed,
We will leave him burst and broken
To go down among the damned.

Shake Out Your Banners

Come, shake out your banners, and forth
    to the fight,
Joy, joy to our heart that this day we
    have seen,
When the war-flags of Labour, saluting
    the light
Of Freedom for mankind, around us doth
    stream;
Oh, the tyrants may quake lest the blood
    they have poured
O'er the fields of the earth their crowns
    to be-gem,
May rise to our thoughts as we unsheathe
    the sword,
And harden our hearts 'gainst the spoilers
    of men.

Ay, the sword glitters grandly, but not as
    of yore.
When brother smote brother in murderous
    feud,
Or the nod of a tyrant rushed nations to
    war,
And the hopes of our race were o'erwhelmed
    in blood.
Nay, the fight that we fight is a fight for
    our own,
And "Freedom for Labour" our war's tocsin
    shall be,
Through the broad earth resounding, till
    Capital's throne
Lies shattered for aye, and the toiler is
    free.

Saoirse a Rúin

Thou, saviour yet to be,
    Saoirse, a rúin!
Dearer than life to me,
    Saoirse, a rúin!
May all I give to thee,
Grant that mine eyes may see
Thee in thy majesty,
    Saoirse, a rúin!
Hard was our travail past,
    Saoirse, a rúin!
Long held in bondage fast,
    Saoirse, a rúin!
Weary the road we've passed,
By error's clouds o'ercast,
Thy light breaks in at last,
    Saoirse, a rúin!

Oft hath our master's tongue,
    Saoirse, a rúin!
Glibly thy glories sung,
    Saoirse, a rúin!
Loudly thy harp they've strung,
Wildly thy praises flung—
    Saoirse, a rúin!

Long have we sought thy light,
    Saoirse, a rúin!
Through Oppression's darkest night
    Saoirse, a rúin!
And ne'er shall cease the fight
'Gainst the tyrant's hateful might,
Till thou shalt bless our sight,
    Saoirse, a rúin!
Forth, then we march to-day,
    Freedom our own!
Eager, panting for the fray,
    Freedom our own!
'Neath thy sun's enlight'ning ray
Naught shall our progress stay,
Soon thou shall reign alway,
    Freedom our own!

A Father in Exile
Written by James Connolly in the U.S., Christmas, 1903

'Tis Christmas Day in Ireland,
    And I'm sitting here alone,
Three thousand miles of ocean intervene,
And the faces of my loved ones
    In my little Irish home
Come glancing in and out my thoughts between;
O, to catch the loving kisses
    From my little children flung,
To feel the warm embrace when wife
    And husband meet,
To hear the boisterous greeting in
    The kindly Dublin tongue
That makes brightness of the dullness
    Of our murky Dublin streets.

'Tis Christmas Day in Ireland,
    And I, my lot bewailing,
Am fretting in this Western land, so cold,
Where the throbbings of the human heart
    Are weak and unavailing,
And human souls are reckoned less than gold;
O, the headache and the heartache
    And the ashes at the feast
Attend us every hour of our sojourn
    In this land,
Till the heart-sick Irish exile turns
    His face towards the East,
To that land where love and poverty
    Can wander hand in hand.

'Tis Christmas Day in Ireland,
    And ringing over yonder
Are Dublin streets with Irish love of life,
And I'm here in exile moping,
    In spirit yearning wander
To that Irish land to meet my Irish wife
O, the lovings and the strivings and the
    Griefs we share in common,
And the babes that came to bless us
    As sweet buds upon a tree,
O, curses on the cruel fate that sent
    A father roaming,
And blessings still this Christmastide
    My Irish home on thee.

A Festive Song

    Comrades, clasp hands,
    The time demands
This night we spend enjoying
    The jovial word
    Round festive board,
Grim, carking care destroying.
    Liquor this night
    Shall sparkle bright,
With homage pay to Beauty,
    And brave men who
    Oft conflict knew,
Shall take a rest from duty.

CHORUS
    Then fill the cup
    With liquor up,
Pledge ev'ry man his neighbour,
    That in the light
    Of Truth he'll fight
To win the world for Labour.

    Comrades, the tears
    Our Class thro' years
Hath shed the wide world over,
    Have taken root,
    And soon the fruit
Our tyrants shall discover;
    And when at length
    We show our strength,
And send each despot flying,
    With joy and mirth,
    Like ours, the Earth
Shall hail Oppression dying.

CHORUS

    For who with zest
    Can laugh the best
But he who laughs the longest
    And in the fight
    'Twixt wrong and right
The laugh is with the strongest;
    Since Time began
    Fate's mighty plan
The laugh gave to the proudest

But History
Shall tell that we
Did laugh the last and loudest.

Chorus

Then, comrades, toast
Great Freedom's host,
And loudly sing her praises,
And honoured be,
O'er land and sea,
Woe'er her banner raises,
So, ere we leave,
A wreath we'll weave
Of flow'rs of Earth's best gleaning
With Maid and Wife,
With Hope of Life
Free from a tyrant's scheming.

Chorus

After Ireland is free, says the patriot who won't touch socialism, we will protect all classes, and if you won't pay your rent
you will be evicted same as now. But the evicting party, under
command of the sheriff, will wear green uniforms and the Harp
without the Crown, and the warrant turning you out on the
roadside will be stamped with the arms of the Irish Republic.
—James Connolly

James Connolly
Maeve Cavanagh

Genius was his—prescience, changeless aim,
   In conscious power he wrought his life's
     great task!
Chose his own hour, contemptuous of Fame,
His very name he left the world to ask.

Alas! that Ireland knew him late—so late,
   And in the tragic hour of sacrifice;
Knew for her sake, he made his own high
     fate—
   Ransomed her soul and gladly paid the
     price.

Where lies his grave, no hand may Laurel
     place,
   There prison walls throw down their
     shadow grim;
But it will be a shrine where all his race
   In days of doubt will turn and learn of him.

Ireland as distinct from her people, is nothing to me: and the man who is bubbling over with love and enthusiasm for "Ireland," and can yet pass unmoved through our streets and witness all the wrong and the suffering, the shame and the degradation wrought upon the people of Ireland—aye, wrought by Irishmen upon Irishmen and women, without burning to end it, is in my opinion, a fraud and a liar in his heart, no matter how he loves that combination of chemical elements he is pleased to call "Ireland."
     —James Connolly

James Connolly, New York, September 1902.

Irish Citizen Army outside the original Liberty Hall, Dublin, Ireland, 1914. The banner, "We serve neither King nor Kaiser," was put up when Connolly became acting general secretary of the ITGWU (Irish Transport and General Workers' Union) following James Larkin's departure for America in October 1914.

Under the Auspices of the Irish Socialist Federation

A FAREWELL DINNER

TO

James Connolly

National Organizer Socialist Party of Ireland, Editor The "Harp"

GOOD SPEAKERS

**THURSDAY,
JULY 14th,
1910
7.30 P. M.**

*Come, bring your
friends. You will
enjoy yourself.*

A FEAST OF MIRTH

**THURSDAY,
JULY 14th,
1910
7.30 P. M.**

*A night of Real
Irish song and
story.*

CAVANAGH'S RESTAURANT
258 WEST 23RD STREET, NEAR 8TH AVE.
TICKET . . . . . . ONE DOLLAR

Tickets may be secured from The Secretary, Connolly Dinner Committee, 749 Third Avenue, New York City.

DON'T MISS THIS OCCASION TO TELL CONNOLLY WHAT YOU THINK OF HIM.

Connolly immigrated to the U.S. in 1903 and joined the Industrial Workers of the World (IWW) in 1905. In 1908 he founded *The Harp* newspaper. The above announces his farewell dinner as he readies to depart New York and return to Dublin, 14 July 1910.

Below: The Flag of the Irish Citizen Army, often referred to as the Starry Plough.

Early recruits to the Irish Citizen Army drilling in Phoenix Park, Dublin, in December 1913. James Connolly is second from the right.

James Connolly and his wife, Lillie, and daughters, Mona and Nora. Edinburgh, Scotland, c. 1895.

Speaking on the Fiery Cross tour. In back: "Big" Jim Larkin and James Connolly. In front: Mrs Bamber (Liverpool Trades Council) and "Big" Bill Haywood (Industrial Workers of the World).

Bibliography

EDITOR'S NOTE: Connolly's writings are readily available via the internet and in books. The websites listed below are an excellent place to begin. In a large and growing body of literature, three books are, in my view, required reading: *James Connolly Selected Writings*, edited by P. Beresford Ellis, *Portrait of a Rebel Father* by Nora Connolly O'Brien, and *The Life and Times of James Connolly* by C. Desmond Greaves.

Connolly's Own Books and Pamphlets:

Erin's Hope: The End and the Means, first published by the Irish Socialist Republican Party, March 1897.
Socialism and Nationalism, 1897.
The New Evangel, 1901.
Socialism Made Easy, first published by C.H. Kerr & Co., Chicago, 1908.
Labour, Nationality and Religion, The Harp Library, Dublin, August 1910.
Labour In Irish History, Maunsel & Co., Dublin, November 1910.
The Reconquest of Ireland, Liberty Hall, Dublin, 1915.

Selections and Collections:

James Connolly, Collected Works (2 vols), New Books Publications, Dublin, 1987.

The Lost Writings, James Connolly, Pluto Press, London, 1997.

James Connolly: Selected Writings, edited by P. Beresford Ellis, Pluto Press, London, 1988.

The Words of James Connolly, edited by James Connolly Heron, Mercier Press, Cork, 1986.

James Connolly: A Full Life, Donal Nevin, Gill & Macmillan, Dublin, 2005.

The Workers' Republic, NuVision Publishers, Sioux Falls, SD, 2007.

James Connolly, Between Comrades: Letters and Correspondence 1889–1916, edited by Donal Nevin, Gill & Macmillan, Dublin, 2007.

Biography and Studies:

Desmond Ryan, *James Connolly: His Life, Work & Writings*, Talbot Press, Dublin, 1924.

Nora Connolly O'Brien, *Portrait of a Rebel Father*, Talbot Press, Dublin, 1935.

Emmet O'Connor, *A Labour History of Ireland, 1824–2000*, University College Dublin Press, Dublin, 2011.

Cathal O'Shannon (ed), *Fifty Years of Liberty Hall*, The Sign of the Three Candles, Dublin, 1959.

Desmond Ryan, "James Connolly," in J.W. Boyle (ed), *Leaders and Workers*, Mercier Press, Cork, 1960; repr. Cork, 1978.

C. Desmond Greaves, *The Life and Times of James Connolly*, Lawrence & Wishart, London, 1961.

Samuel Levenson, *James Connolly: A Biography*, Martin Brian and O'Keeffe, London, 1973.

Roger Faligot, *James Connolly et le mouvement révolutionnaire irlandais*, F. Maspero, Paris, 1978.

Kieran Allen, *The Politics of James Connolly*, Pluto Press, London, 1990.

William K. Anderson, *James Connolly and the Irish Left*, Irish Academic Press, Dublin, 1994.

R.M. Fox, *The History of the Irish Citizen Army*, J. Duffy & Co., Dublin, 1943.

David Lynch, *Radical Politics in Modern Ireland: The Irish Socialist Republican Party 1896–1904*, Irish Academic Press, Dublin, 2005.

Carl Reeve and Ann Barton Reeve, *James Connolly and the United States: The Road to the 1916 Irish Rebellion*, Humanities Press, Atlantic Highland New Jersey, 1978.

Fintan Lane, *The Origins of Modern Irish Socialism, 1881–1896*, Cork University Press, Cork, 1997.

Online:

CELT (Corpus of Electronic Texts)—http://celt.ucc.ie

Marxists Internet Archive—http://www.marxists.org/archive/connolly/

James Connolly Society—http://www.wageslave.org/jcs/

The Hidden Connolly—http://www.redbannermagazine.com/hiddenconnolly.htm

Drawing of Connolly by Seán O'Sullivan, Royal Hibernian Academy.

Acknowledgments

P ROJECTS SUCH AS this depend on many people making a collective effort. Contributions of practical assistance, learned advice, organizational skill, and financial resources came from diverse individuals and groups, in Ireland, the United States, and Switzerland.

Markus Steck
Mark Stenzler
Chris Carlsson
Claude Marks
Csaba Polony
Des McGuinness
Frank Allen
Sean Prendiville
Jim Lane
James Connolly Heron
Theo Dorgan
Des Geraghty
Padraig Yeates
Renee Gibbons
Margaret Cooley
Alan Fung
Edith Eckhart
Dan McGinley

Joe Mulheron
Jonathan Melrod
Pete Kelly
Lizzy McHugh
Jimmy Dignam
Joe Higgins
Frank Connolly
Antoinette McKenna (RIP)
Joe McKenna
Tony Browne
Mike Bartlett
Declan Gallagher
Ciaran Gallagher
Mary Gallagher
Aveen Sproule
Andy Sproule
Tomás O'Riordan

Institutions and organizations

ILWU Local 34
Canton Bern
Canton Schaffhausen
City of Bern
Burgergemeinde Bern
The Arlene Francis Center, Santa Rosa, CA.

Special thanks to Yvonne Moore for her tireless effort raising the funds and handling the administration for this project.

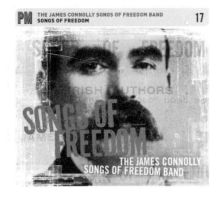

SONGS OF FREEDOM
The James Connolly Songs of Freedom Band

$14.95 · CD
ISBN: 978-1-60486-826-5

From the rollicking welcome of "A Festive Song" to the defiant battle cry of "Watchword of Labor," *Songs of Freedom* accomplishes the difficult task of making contemporary music out of old revolutionary songs. Far from the archival preservation of embalmed corpses, the inspired performance of a rocking band turns the timeless lyrics of James Connolly into timely manifestos for today's young rebels. As Connolly himself repeatedly urged, nothing can replace the power of music to raise the fighting spirit of the oppressed.

Giving expression to Connolly's internationalism, musical influences ranging from traditional Irish airs to American rhythm and blues are combined here in refreshing creativity. As for the songs themselves, nine have lyrics by Connolly, three were written about Connolly, and one, "The Red Flag," was chosen by Connolly to be in the original *Songs of Freedom* songbook of 1907, subsequently becoming a classic song of Labor. The instrumentation is acoustic: guitars, uilleann pipes, whistles, fiddle, accordion, and Irish harp, as well as drums and bass.

1. A Festive Song
2. Be Moderate
3. Human Freedom
4. Connolly Was There
5. A Rebel Song
6. Saoirse a Rúin
7. When Labor Calls
8. O Slaves of Toil
9. Shake Out Your Banners
10. James Connolly the Irish Rebel
11. The Red Flag
12. Watchword of Labor
13. Where Is James Connolly?

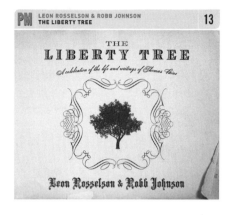

LEON ROSSELSON & ROBB JOHNSON
THE LIBERTY TREE

13

THE
LIBERTY TREE
A celebration of the life and writings of Thomas Paine

Leon Rosselson & Robb Johnson

THE LIBERTY TREE: A CELEBRATION OF THE LIFE AND WRITINGS OF THOMAS PAINE

Leon Rosselson and Robb Johnson

$20.00 · 2xCD & booklet

ISBN: 978-1-60486-339-0

The Liberty Tree tells the story of Tom Paine's extraordinary life, interweaving Paine's own words, from his letters and the pamphlets which made him one of the most influential and dangerous writers of his age, with extracts from newspaper reports, diaries, letters, and other documents of the times. The songs of Robb Johnson and Leon Rosselson add another dimension to the story, reflecting Paine's radical ideas and evaluating them in the context of the 21st century. This unique blend of words and music challenges received opinion in the same way Paine's writings did.

LEON ROSSELSON
THE WORLD TURNED UPSIDE DOWN

14

LEON ROSSELSON
The World Turned Upside Down
Rosselsongs 1960-2010

"The man is a songwriting colossus" –fRoots

THE WORLD TURNED UPSIDE DOWN: ROSSELSONGS 1960–2010

Leon Rosselson

$44.95 · 4xCD & booklet

ISBN: 978-1-60486-498-4

The life and times of England's greatest living songwriter are captured in a deluxe box set containing 72 songs on 4 CDs and an 80-page book.

Frankie Armstrong, Roy Bailey, Mark Bassey, Steve Berry, Billy Bragg, Martin Carthy, Howard Evans, Clare Lintott, Chris Foster, Sue Harris, Paul Jayasinha, Sianed Jones, John Kirkpatrick, Elizabeth Mansfield, Ruth Rosselson, Fiz Shapur, Dave Swarbrick, Miranda Sykes, Roger Williams, The 3 City 4, The Oyster Band, and The Sheffield Socialist Choir all contribute variously to the songs too, in one form or another.

SOCIALIST AND LABOR SONGS: AN INTERNATIONAL REVOLUTIONARY SONGBOOK
Edited by Elizabeth Morgan
Preface by Utah Phillips
$14.95 · ISBN: 978-1-60486-392-5

Seventy-seven songs—with words and sheet music—of solidarity, revolt, humor, and revolution. Compiled from several generations in America, and from around the world, they were originally written in English, Danish, French, German, Italian, Spanish, Russian, and Yiddish.

From IWW anthems such as "The Preacher and the Slave" to Lenin's favorite 1905 revolutionary anthem "Whirlwinds of Danger," many works by the world's greatest radical songwriters are anthologized herein: Edith Berkowitz, Bertolt Brecht, Ralph Chaplin, James Connolly, Havelock Ellis, Emily Fine, Arturo Giovannitti, Joe Hill, Langston Hughes, William Morris, James Oppenheim, Teresina Rowell, Anna Garlin Spencer, Maurice Sugar—and dozens more.

ENGLISH REBEL SONGS 1381–1984
Chumbawamba
$14.95 · CD · ISBN: 978-1-60486-000-9

English Rebel Songs 1381–1984 is Chumbawamba's homage to the men and women who never had obituaries in the broadsheets. This is an album that conjures up the tragedies and triumphs of the people who shaped England: its citizens. This album was originally recorded in 1988 when Chumbawamba was determined to stir up a rout in the tiny anarcho-punk community by swapping guitars and drums for a cappella singing. The songs were discovered in songbooks, in folk clubs, and on cassette tapes. This CD is guaranteed to sway the listener, break hearts, and encourage hope... just as those who inspired the songs by changing history.

REBEL VOICES: AN IWW ANTHOLOGY
Edited by Joyce L. Kornbluh
Preface by Daniel Gross
Contributions by Franklin
Rosemont
Introduction by Fred Thompson
$27.95 · ISBN: 978-1-60486-483-0

Welcoming women, Blacks, and immigrants
long before most other unions, the Wobblies
from the start were labor's outstanding pioneers
and innovators, unionizing hundreds of thou-
sands of workers previously regarded as "unorganizable." Wobblies organized the
first sit-down strike (at General Electric, Schenectady, 1906), the first major auto
strike (6,000 Studebaker workers, Detroit, 1911), the first strike to shut down all
three coalfields in Colorado (1927), and the first "no-fare" transit-workers' job-action
(Cleveland, 1944). With their imaginative, colorful, and world-famous strikes and
free-speech fights, the IWW wrote many of the brightest pages in the annals of
working class emancipation.

Wobblies also made immense and invaluable contributions to workers' culture. All
but a few of America's most popular labor songs are Wobbly songs. IWW cartoons
have long been recognized as labor's finest and funniest.

The impact of the IWW has reverberated far beyond the ranks of organized labor.
An important influence on the 1960s New Left, the Wobbly theory and practice of
direct action, solidarity, and "class-war" humor have inspired several generations
of civil rights and antiwar activists, and are a major source of ideas and inspiration
for today's radicals. Indeed, virtually every movement seeking to "make this planet
a good place to live" (to quote an old Wobbly slogan), has drawn on the IWW's
incomparable experience.

Originally published in 1964 and long out of print, *Rebel Voices* remains by far the
biggest and best source on IWW history, fiction, songs, art, and lore. This new edition includes 40 pages of additional material from the 1998 Charles H. Kerr edition
from Fred Thompson and Franklin Rosemont, and a new preface by Wobbly organizer Daniel Gross.

About
PM Press

PM Press was founded at the end of 2007 by a small collection of folks with decades of publishing, media, and organizing experience. PM Press co-conspirators have published and distributed hundreds of books, pamphlets, CDs, and DVDs. Members of PM have founded enduring book fairs, spearheaded victorious tenant organizing campaigns, and worked closely with bookstores, academic conferences, and even rock bands to deliver political and challenging ideas to all walks of life. We're old enough to know what we're doing and young enough to know what's at stake.

We seek to create radical and stimulating fiction and non-fiction books, pamphlets, T-shirts, visual and audio materials to entertain, educate and inspire you. We aim to distribute these through every available channel with every available technology—whether that means you are seeing anarchist classics at our bookfair stalls; reading our latest vegan cookbook at the café; downloading geeky fiction e-books; or digging new music and timely videos from our website.

PM Press is always on the lookout for talented and skilled volunteers, artists, activists and writers to work with. If you have a great idea for a project or can contribute in some way, please get in touch.

PM Press • PO Box 23912 • Oakland, CA 94623
510-658-3906 • info@pmpress.org

Buy books and stay on top of what we are doing at:

www.pmpress.org

FOPM

MONTHLY SUBSCRIPTION PROGRAM

These are indisputably momentous times—the financial system is melting down globally and the Empire is stumbling. Now more than ever there is a vital need for radical ideas.

In the six years since its founding—and on a mere shoestring—PM Press has risen to the formidable challenge of publishing and distributing knowledge and entertainment for the struggles ahead. With over 250 releases to date, we have published an impressive and stimulating array of literature, art, music, politics, and culture. Using every available medium, we've succeeded in connecting those hungry for ideas and information to those putting them into practice.

Friends of PM allows you to directly help impact, amplify, and revitalize the discourse and actions of radical writers, filmmakers, and artists. It provides us with a stable foundation from which we can build upon our early successes and provides a much-needed subsidy for the materials that can't necessarily pay their own way. You can help make that happen—and receive every new title automatically delivered to your door once a month—by joining as a Friend of PM Press. And, we'll throw in a free T-shirt when you sign up.

Here are your options:

- $30 a month: Get all books and pamphlets plus 50% discount on all webstore purchases
- $40 a month: Get all PM Press releases (including CDs and DVDs) plus 50% discount on all webstore purchases
- $100 a month: Superstar—Everything plus PM merchandise, free downloads, and 50% discount on all webstore purchases

For those who can't afford $30 or more a month, we're introducing Sustainer Rates at $15, $10, and $5. Sustainers get a free PM Press T-shirt and a 50% discount on all purchases from our website.

Your Visa or Mastercard will be billed once a month, until you tell us to stop. Or until our efforts succeed in bringing the revolution around. Or the financial meltdown of Capital makes plastic redundant. Whichever comes first.